DATE DUE

DE 30'93			
MAR 0 6 1998			
MAY 2 5 2001			

PATTERN
IN EARLY CHRISTIAN WORSHIP

PATTERN
IN EARLY CHRISTIAN WORSHIP

■■■

Allen Cabaniss

■■■

ISBN 0-86554-345-3

PATTERN
IN EARLY CHRISTIAN WORSHIP
Copyright © 1989
Mercer University Press
Macon, Georgia 31207
All rights reserved
Printed in the United States of America

LIBRARY OF CONGRESS
CATALOGING-IN-PUBLICATION DATA

Cabaniss, Allen, 1911–
Pattern in early Christian worship / Allen Cabaniss.
x + 112 pp.   15x23 cm.   6x9 in.
Bibliography : pp. 93-101.
Includes indexes.
ISBN 0-86554-345-3 (alk. paper)
1. Liturgics—History. I. Title.
BV185.C33   1989   89-2254
264'.009'015—dc19   CIP

CONTENTS

DEDICATION

For
LAUREN ELIZABETH
and
BRITTANY ANNE

ACKNOWLEDGMENTS

THE NOTES TO THE TEXT of the ensuing essays will make suitable acknowledgement of some previous works. Several, however, require special mention here: Oscar Cullmann, *Early Christian Worship,* trans. A. S. Todd and J. B. Torrance (London: SCM Press, 1954); R. P. Martin, *Worship in the Early Church* (Grand Rapids MI: W. B. Eerdmans Publishing Co., 1975; first published in 1964); and Ferdinand Hahn, *The Worship of the Early Church,* trans. D. E. Green, ed. John Reumann (Philadelphia: Fortress Press, 1975); all of them disparate in approach. I might add E. P. Martin's *The Worship of God* (Grand Rapids MI: W. B. Eerdmans Publishing Co., 1982) but for the fact that, however excellent his first eleven chapters, he proposes in chapter 12 an *ordo* that "breaks with the early tradition" so severely as to suggest that he has forgotten his own previous research. H. O. Old, *Worship* (Atlanta: John Knox Press, 1984), in the series "Guides to the Reformed Tradition," is an excellent "guide" but not concerned with the "pattern."

There is no way adequately to recognize the tutelage of one's professors, but I single out two church historians: the Rev. Prof. John T. McNeill, an ecumenical Presbyterian who directed my doctoral studies, and the Rev. Prof. Andrew K. Rule, a conservative Presbyterian who supervised my seminary training, both now deceased: *requiescant in pace.* Although not professional liturgiologists, they were knowledgeable in the area, sympathetic, and helpful.

My special thanks are due the following for permission to use copyrighted material.

The University of Chicago Press, for employing (with additions, deviations, and deletions) my essay, "Liturgy-Making Factors in Primitive Christianity," *Journal of Religion* 23 (1945): 43-58, in chapters 3 and 4 below;

The Cambridge University Press, New Rochelle, New York, for a passage from G. G. Coulton, *Medieval Panorama* (paperback, 1959) pp. 14-15, quoted in chapter 4 below; and

The Living Church, Milwaukee, Wisconsin, H. Boone Porter, editor, for the verses by Bert Penny in the issue of 18 November 1956, p. 11, quoted in chapter 7 below.

My late sister assisted by listening to my original efforts in producing this essay and by typing early drafts. My latest relatives, two darling great-great-nieces, add to my work by providing an element of playful distraction—to them with "major-avuncular" piety I dedicate this book.

Allen Cabaniss
University, Mississippi

PROLOGUE

I DO NOT RECALL A TIME when I was not influenced by liturgy; it has been a golden thread stretching from an unremembered past into the present. Not only the practice, but also the study of it has been a deep-seated interest for me. Much of my research and writing has been involved with *liturgica*.[1] More than a quarter of a century ago I wrote a quasi-popular note on the subject and submitted it to my denominational journal. After needlessly extended consideration, it was finally published in an edited version, with an asterisked remark giving Webster's dictionary definition of *liturgy*, as though the editor did not know or expect the reader to know the term![2] Today the word is bandied about—but with obvious lack of clear understanding.

A young administrative cleric has, for example, declared pontifically, "Worship, in its most profound sense, is coextensive with the

---

[1] See, among others, the following essays: "A Note on the Liturgy of the Apocalypse," *Interpretation* 7 (1953): 78-85; "The Harrowing of Hell, Psalm 24, and Pliny the Younger: a Note," *Vigiliae Christianae* 7 (1953): 65-74; "Wisdom 18:14f.: An early Christmas Text," ibid. 10 (1956): 97-102; "Early Christian Nighttime Worship," *Journal of Bible and Religion* 25 (1957): 30-33; "The Worship of 'Most Primitive' Christianity," ibid. 26 (1958): 318-21; "Alleluia: A Word and Its Effect," *Studies in English* 5 (1964): 67-74; all of them reprinted in my *Liturgy and Literature* (Tuscaloosa: University of Alabama Press, 1970). Other of my essays will be noted below as occasion requires.

[2] "Shields, the Liturgy, and I," *Presbyterian Survey* 46 (March 1956): 41, even omitting reference to it in the table of contents. Ironically, less than three years earlier the same journal (with the same editor) had not hesitated over the same word in my paper, "Doctor Mack on the Liturgy," ibid. 43 (September 1957): 34-35.

entirety of a Christian's life."[3] Like pantheism, which dissipates God into everything, such language makes worship (liturgy) unidentifiable. In order to write his book, however, he narrowed the term to what he called "its popular sense . . . , the familiar group experience on Sunday morning in the sanctuary."[4] This presumed clarification contains no less than three errors. First, his restriction is not the *popular,* but the technical sense. Second, the limitation to Sunday morning is doubly and unnecessarily confining. Third, the church of which he spoke has, in proper theological terminology, no earthly sanctuary (a place where sacrifice is offered), but an auditorium (where the Word of God is read, heard, and expounded).

We live in an era of liturgical experimentation, some of it mere confusion; some, sincere and acceptable aggiornamento. It seems to me that the most important requirement of that activity is to maintain the basic structure inherited from apostolic times. Regardless of how far we proceed in modernizing the language, we should keep the rationale of what has come down to us. The old dictum, *lex orandi lex credendi* (worship and belief are intimately related),[5] should be upheld: how we pray should reflect our belief and what we believe should be expressed in our worship. If we disjoin the two we make our worship mendacious and our faith intangible. So it is always well to seek again the source and to embrace it heartily.

[3]Julius Melton, *Presbyterian Worship in America* (Richmond VA: John Knox Press, 1967) 9.

[4]Ibid. Melton failed to notice several of my articles obviously pertinent to his research: "Liturgy in the Southern Presbyterian Church," *Union Seminary Review* 54 (1942): 11-27; "A Critical Review of the *Book of Common Worship* (1946)," *Journal of the Presbyterian Historical Society* 26 (1948): 87-100; "Doctor Mack on the Liturgy" (see n. 2 above); "A Critique of 'Service for the Lord's Day'," *Reformed Liturgics* 1 (Fall 1964): 19-24; "Worship Tested by History," *Presbyterian Outlook* 137 (15 August 1955), 5-6; "In Defense of Liturgy," ibid. 146 (15 June 1964): 2.

[5]A modern treatment of this motif is D. R. Mason, "An Examination of 'Worship' as a Key for Reexamining the God Problem," *Journal of Religion* 55 (1975): 76-94.

CHAPTER 1

THE EARLIEST ACCOUNT
OF CHRISTIAN LITURGY

INQUIRY ABOUT PRIMITIVE Christian worship should obviously begin with the earliest unequivocal description of it. Happily that is available in the (First) *Apology* of Justin Martyr about A.D. 155 (chh. 65-67).[1] Although of Palestinian origin, Justin wrote his *Apology* in Rome for Roman hearers, specifically Emperor Antoninus Pius (who reigned 138-161), and his adopted sons Verissimus (the fu-

---

[1]On Justin's account, see the analysis by Richardson in Hans Lietzmann, *Mass and Lord's Supper: A Study in the History of Liturgy,* trans. D. H. G. Reeve, with introduction and further inquiry by R. D. Richardson (Leiden: Brill, 1979) 237-46 and passim; Gregory Dix, *The Shape of the Liturgy,* with additional notes by Paul V. Marshall (New York: Seabury Press, 1982; first published 1945) 222-23; on Justin and his *Apology,* Philip Carrington, *The Early Christian Church* (Cambridge: University Press, 1957) 2:98-121; E. J. Goodspeed, *A History of Early Christian Literature* (Chicago: University of Chicago Press, 1942) 141-57.

Probably the most accessible edition of Justin's *Apology* is the old one by B. L. Gildersleeve, ed., *The Apologies of Justin Martyr* (New York: Harper, 1877), wherein the (First) *Apology* is presented on pp. 3-65. Of that edition Goodspeed apparently thought well (see his *History of Christian Literature,* 304), although no reference to it occurred in E. J. Goodspeed, *A History of Early Christian Literature,* rev. and enlarged by R. M. Grant (Chicago: University of Chicago Press, 1966), probably owing to the age of Gildersleeve's edition. There are numerous translations of the liturgical passages of the *Apology.* I have made internal references to the relevant chapters (*Apol.*) and to his *Dialogue with Trypho (Dial.).* All translations herein are my own.

ture Marcus Aurelius) and Lucius. As indicated by its title the trea-
tise is a defense of Christianity against prevalent
misunderstandings. Consequently Justin employed terms that his
pagan audience would comprehend; or he explained when he used
an occasional technical expression. One must, therefore, not expect
to discover in his remarks about liturgy certain terms that later become commonplace, at least among specialists in such study.

The first fact to be noted is Justin's careful indication of the day
of worship. The Christian assembly took place on the day of Helios
(the sun, or perhaps the sun god), particularly identified both as the
day following that of Kronos (Saturn) and as being the first day of
the week. Creation of the world as well as the resurrection of Messiah were given as reasons for observing that day (67). At that time
all the believers gathered together "at the same place" (*epi to auto;*
cf. 1 Cor. 11:20; 14:23; Acts 2:1; 4:5), but the particular kind of
place was not identified, nor the particular time of day or night (67).

The second point to be made relates to composition of the
assembly: it was one of persons called "brothers" (65), of city-
dwellers and those of the countryside, of well-to-do and poor alike,
of "the people" (65, 67; *ho laos*). It was a band of persons deeply
interested in each other's welfare. The more affluent took care of
needy ones by presenting collections of voluntary contributions to
the leader, who then distributed to orphans, widows, the sick, cap-
tives (or prisoners), and sojourners (67). It was also a group of people who, however far removed from Palestine geographically or
temperamentally, could and did employ "enthusiastically" a peculiarly Hebraic expression, the *Amen* (65, 67).

Above all, it was an assembly of likeminded people who
assented to the truth of what they had been taught, who had
received the washing for remission of sins and for rebirth, and who
lived according to what Messiah had handed down (66). Part of the
truth in which they had been instructed was elaborated by Justin
as belief in God, Father and Creator of all, His Son Jesus Messiah,
and the Holy Spirit (65, 67); as belief that Jesus Messiah was savior
and that by God's Word He had been made flesh (66, 67); as belief

that He had been crucified on one Friday, but on the following Sunday He rose from the dead, appeared to His apostles and students, and taught them (67). The apostles, in their memoirs called "gospels," thereupon transmitted the tradition that Jesus took bread, offered thanksgiving, gave it to them with the words, "This is my body" (preceded by the command, "Do this for *anamnesis* of me"); and similarly took the cup, offered thanksgiving, and gave it to them with the words, "This is my blood," without reference to *anamnesis* (66).

A third observation should be made, namely, regarding organization of the assembly. As indicated, the whole group was denominated "brothers" or "the people." There was, however, a presiding official called the *proestos* (65, 67), perhaps "director" or "manager." He was also called *kedemon* (67), the "caretaker" (of those in need and of funds collected for their benefit). The "president" had assistants in the service called "deacons" (65, 67). There was also a person who read aloud the apostolic and prophetic writings at the service: he was called the *anaginoskon* (reader or lector).

Before analyzing the description of Justin's service, we may ask if what has already been set forth has biblical antecedents. It is noteworthy that Justin felt it needful to explain only four terms that he employed. (1) The assembly was made up of "those called brothers." The word *brothers* was often used in the New Testament to designate members of the Christian church (e.g., 1 Cor. 1:10 and frequently elsewhere). The assembly was otherwise described as *ho laos* (65, 67) with probable allusion to such passages as Heb. 2:17; 4:9; and 1 Pet. 2:9-10. (2) "In the Hebrew tongue the Amen means, 'May it be (so),' " or an emphatic "Yes!" It was an expression of assent in response to prayer, for example, in 1 Cor. 14:16; 2 Cor. 1:20; Rev. 1:6-7. (3) The apostles had produced memoirs "which are called gospels." The term *gospel* was employed in pagan literature to mean "good news," but, as here in Justin, also meant written books (note the plural) conveying God's good news (cf. Mark 1:1). (4) Justin's phrase, "those who are called deacons among us," also takes up a word of common usage meaning *servants* and gives it a particular Christian significance, as used by Paul in the sense of *assistants* to bishops (Phil. 1:1; cf. 1 Tim. 3:8-10).

The "collection" (*sullegomenon*) is a term which harks back to a related one (*logeia*) employed by Paul for virtually the same purpose (1 Cor. 16:1 and elsewhere). The reference to "orphans and widows" among the needy recalls, *for example,* the wording of Jas. 1:27. The word *washing* (*loutron*) for baptism is the same usage as in Eph. 5:26 (a cleansing with water through the Word) and Tit. 3:5 (a washing of rebirth and renewal by the Holy Spirit). The mention of the three Persons of the Trinity is obviously of scriptural origin (cf. Matt. 28:19; 2 Cor. 13:14), as also is the assertion of the Incarnation (John 1:14; 1 John 4:2). The historical data of Friday as day of the crucifixion and Sunday as day of the resurrection of Jesus conform to biblical evidence (cf. Mark 15:42; 16:1-2; and parallels). The recital of the Eucharistic institution is not an exact quotation of any extant gospel or of Paul's narrative in 1 Cor. 11:23-25, although it is clearly related to them, especially to Mark. The word *anamnesis,* however, is Pauline.

The term *proestos* for leader of the brothers is interesting. The word *bishop* or *pastor* was available by Justin's time, but he chose not to employ it. Curiously enough the Latin-English term *president,* which is an appropriate translation, is etymologically different. To be slavishly literal it means "one who sits (in front)" or "chairman," while *proestos* suggests "one who stands (in front)." But the Greek is anticipated in 1 Thess. 5:12 (*proistamenous,* "those put over you"), 1 Tim. 3:4 (*proistamenon,* a good "manager"), 1 Tim. 5:17 (*hoi kalos proestotes presbuteroi,* "the presbyters who are good directors"), and elsewhere. The way *kedemon* is used has nonverbal antecedents in Jas. 1:27 and 1 Pet. 5:1-2 with their suggestion of *bishop, presbyter, pastor.* Finally, the word *anaginoskon* (reader, lector) is anticipated by the same usage in Mark 13:14 ‖ Matt. 24:15 and Rev. 1:3.

Thus far at no less than fourteen points does Justin's terminology or meaning have clear New Testament antecedents. Only the first four of them required some explanation to the author's pagan audience. The other ten Justin felt would be clear enough, because he was using language they could understand, albeit based on sufficient New Testament authority. It is interesting that he did not use *bishop,* although the term was employed by the pagan world to indicate a person whose function was that of supervision.

Turning now to the service of worship, we note that Justin gave two similar accounts of it: one, following a baptism (65); the other, the ordinary Sunday service (67). It began with a lector reading from the memoirs of the apostles (67; that is, the gospels, 66) or from books of the prophets (67). By the time of Justin there were in existence several gospels, hence the plural usage. It has been suggested that the "prophets" were Christian prophets. It may be so, but the implication is certainly of the Old Testament prophets (cf. Rom. 16:26). In any case the reading was done by a special official distinct from the *proestos* and the deacons. The reading continued as long as time permitted, so we get a picture of lengthy portions of the holy writings.

When the lector finished his part of the service, the *proestos* made a discourse admonishing (cf. 1 Thess. 5:12) and urging imitation of those good examples. Then all stood up together and offered prayers (67; or, all stood up and offered prayers together). That statement may (but only *may*) imply some kind of sequence of prayers with congregational responses. In the service after a baptism (65) those prayers were specified as for themselves, for the newly admitted member, and for all people everywhere, "that we who have learned the truth may be deemed worthy and be found, through (our) deeds, to be good citizens and keepers of the commandments, that we may be saved with an everlasting salvation" (65).

The characterization of the newly admitted brother as an "enlightened" one is reminiscent of Heb. 6:4; 10:32; and Eph. 5:8. Prayer for all people everywhere suggests 1 Tim. 2:1, 8. "Good citizens" was probably understood by Justin's audience to mean good citizens of the Roman empire, but it would equally well mean good citizens of the realm of God. "Keepers of the commandments" is a thoroughly biblical concept, but it may also be understood as "law-abiding" people in the civil sense. The phrase, "saved with an everlasting salvation," goes back to the prophet, Isa. 45:17, the only use of that peculiar expression in Scripture.

The foregoing prayers were primarily intercession; they clearly marked a division of Justin's picture of the service, which part thus consisted of Scripture, exhortation, and intercessory prayer. Thereafter, wrote Justin, "We greet each other with a kiss" (65), a practice with antecedents noted in Rom. 16:16; 1 Cor. 16:20; 2 Cor. 13:12; 1 Pet. 5:14. In the Pauline passages it is called a "holy" kiss; in the Petrine, a kiss "of love." That was followed by a presentation—to the *proestos*—of bread (65, 66, 67; *artos,* the same word as used by the first three Evangelists and Paul: Matt. 26:26 ‖ Mark 14:22 ‖ Luke 22:19; 1 Cor. 11:23, cf. 10:16) and what is variously called "a cup of water and watered wine" (*krama,* 65), or "wine and water" (65, 67), or "drink," or "a cup" (62, *poma, poterion*). Interestingly the biblical references do not state "wine" unequivocally, but "cup" and "fruit of the vine" (Matt. 26:27, 29 ‖ Mark 14:23, 25 ‖ Luke 22:17, 18; Paul simply says "cup," 1 Cor. 11:25, cf. 10:16).

Taking the elements brought to him, the *proestos* "sends up" prayers and thanksgivings (67), specifically praise and glory to the Father of all through the name of the Son and the Holy Spirit (cf. 1 Cor. 6:11) and thanksgiving that "we have been deemed worthy of those things" (65). One place says that he made this prayer "at some length" (65); another, that he did so "according to his ability" (67). This prayer, then, was both comprehensive and at the discretion of the *proestos*. It was probably not absolutely fixed; it may have been, at least in part, *extempore;* but the outline and content were sufficiently familiar to the people that they could respond heartily with the ancient Hebrew acclamation *Amen* (65, 67). It is not clear that recital of the narrative of institution (66) was included in the prayer, or indeed in the service.

Then followed distribution of the Eucharistic elements by the deacons and reception or participation by the people. Thus the service came to a close. It remained only for the deacons to carry the elements to those who could not be present (65, 67). The second part of the service had consisted of the kiss of fellowship, presentation of the elements, prayer, and Communion.

As the service stands in the *Apology* of Justin Martyr, one is impressed with its abruptness: without any (recorded) preliminaries it started with lengthy reading of the Scriptures; and without any dismissal ceremony it ended when the people had made their Communion. There is no evidence of singing; there is no mention of place, hour of the day, arrangement of the people, or how long it lasted. Surprisingly there is no reference to breaking the bread, although that was a fairly common biblical term for the Eucharist (Luke 24:35; Acts 2:42, 46; 20:7, 11; 27:35; 1 Cor. 10:16; etc.). There is only one thing unmentioned by Justin that we can confidently assume, namely, the presence of a table, a practical necessity for the service.[2] Strangest of all perhaps to a modern student was Justin's failure to associate the Eucharist with Jesus's death (or with the Jewish Pesach); on the contrary, he associated it rather with His Incarnation (66, twice). Despite Paul's explicit statement that the Communion is a proclamation of Jesus's death (1 Cor. 11:26), none of the Evangelists make such a remark. In fact, like Justin, John 6:32-33, 50-51, 58 may associate it with the Incarnation; and Paul's *anamnesis* statements (1 Cor. 11:24-25) simply refer to a memorial of "me," that is, the total Jesus, not merely His death.

In his chapter between the two descriptions Justin noted that only baptized believers were permitted to partake of the food which was called *eucharist* (thanksgiving) by the Christian community (66). For, as he continued, it was no ordinary bread and drink. Indeed just as Jesus took flesh and blood for our salvation, so, we have been taught, the Eucharistic food, by which our blood and flesh are nourished through a transformation, is the incarnate Jesus' flesh and blood (66), language strongly reminiscent of John 6:33, 51, 53-56.

---

[2]Unless we can suppose a semihumorous symbolic usage as in Virgil, *Aeneid* 7.116, 122-27!

Justin's phrase that the food was made Eucharistic *di' euches logou tou par' autou* (66) is capable of being interpreted at least four ways: (1) "by a prayer of the Word that is from Him" (an invocation of the Logos); (2) "by the Word's prayer that is from Him" (the Lord's Prayer); (3) "by a word of prayer that is from Him" (general or extemporary prayer); (4) "by a formula of prayer that is from Him" (prescribed and, therefore, common prayer). The phrase has some verbal affinity with 1 Tim. 4:4-5, "Everything created by God is noble and nothing received with thanksgiving (*eucharistias*) is unclean, for it is hallowed by God's Word and prayer (*dia logou theou kai enteuxeos*)."

The apparent starkness of the service in Justin is considerably softened in several ways by what may be deemed an element of "mystery." First, there was restriction of the Eucharist: it was not for everyone indiscriminately, but only for those specially prepared by belief, baptism, and morality. Second, by virtue of the service the elements were no longer common, ordinary food, but were in some manner Jesus Himself. Third, the action was done in obedience to a command by Jesus to His apostles, recorded by them and handed down to Justin's generation (66). Fourth, the service caused the food to be Eucharistic (65, 66, 67; "eucharistized," or however we may translate that particular Greek word).

Fifth, there is an astonishing observation by Justin that the service was in some manner comparable to the Mithraic cultus, wherein "as you know or can learn," he said, "bread and a cup of water are served in the ceremonies of initiation with certain words (said) over them." Justin noted very carefully, however, that the Mithraic practice was not original, that it was an imitation of the Christian rite and was inspired by evil demons (66). But his implied comparison certainly causes one to speculate how far such comparison could be pressed. It also reminds one of Paul's similar implied comparison, "You cannot drink the Master's cup and the demons' cup; you cannot partake of the Master's table and the demons' table" (1 Cor. 10:21).

Despite Justin's effort to present an account of the Christian service in terms intelligible to a pagan audience, we cannot help but be impressed by the heavy reliance on scriptural precedents and warrant, expressed or unexpressed—so typical of Justin in all his extant writings. Despite, moreover, the date of his description, approximately a few years after the middle of the second century, we have his intimation that this was the same service with which he was familiar at the time of his conversion to Christianity about 130. It was not something new, but something that was handed down to him from an earlier period (*ta dedidagmena; ho Christos paredoken; edidachthen; paredokan,* 66) and that he in turn was simply handing on (*anedokamen,* 67; cf. 1 Cor. 11:23). He implied, perhaps rightly, that it was a service that antedated the Mithraic mysteries (66).

In his *Dialogue with Trypho,* a Jew, Justin interpreted the prophecy of Mal. 1:11 to refer to the Eucharist as a sacrifice (*Dial.* 41; cf. *Didache* 14:3). But he carefully specified that prayers and thanksgivings made by worthy persons are the only perfect and pleasing sacrifices to God (*Dial.* 117). He also took the words of Isa. 33:16 in allusion to the bread given by Messiah as *anamnesis* of His incarnation and to the cup which He gave for *anamnesis* of His blood when made with Eucharist or thanksgiving (*Dial.* 70). Earlier in his *Apology* Justin observed that God was not in need of blood, libations, and incense offerings; that true praise of God consisted in sending up, "according to our ability," prayers (*pompas*) and hymns as thanks for our creation, the means of health, the kaleidoscopic qualities of things, the alternation of seasons, and petitions for deathless life through faith in Him (13). In that chapter Justin used the expressions, *logo(i) euches kai eucharistias* and *eucharistous ontas dia logou pompas kai humnous,* which he reflected in chapter 66 by the words *di' euches logou.* Dare we translate his term *pompas* as *processions* instead of *prayers?* If so, we have indeed a dramatic picture. But it is not certain that those words apply to his description of the Eucharist.

Justin also gave some intimation about the service of baptism in chapter 61 of the *Apology.* It began with instruction in Christian belief and Christian morality. Before the administration candidates engaged in prayer and fasting in which they were joined by their Christian friends. Then they were conducted to a place where water was available. There they received a washing with water in the name of God the Father, the Savior Jesus Messiah, and the Holy Spirit. As Justin stated, "They were reborn in the same manner of rebirth as that in which we ourselves, too, had been reborn." That action Justin fortified with quotations of John 3:5, Isa. 1:16-20, and the tradition of the apostles (61). According to Justin, this practice, like the Eucharist, was also aped by others who were instigated by demons (62).

CHAPTER 2

LITURGY
AT THE BEGINNING
OF THE SECOND CENTURY

JUSTIN MARTYR'S DESCRIPTION is a picture of Christian worship for pagan hearers in terms comprehensible to such an audience. Almost half a century earlier there was a sketchy summary of Christian worship presented by a Roman governor who had secured his information from several Christian apostates, a few of whom had deserted the church as much as two decades before his document, that is, about A.D. 92. The famous letter of Pliny the Younger, governor of Bithynia and Pontica, was sent both as a report and as an inquiry to Emperor Trajan (who reigned 98-117).[1] In order to be

---

[1]It is letter 96, book 10, of Pliny's correspondence. Letter 97 in Trajan's reply. See S. E. Stout, *Plinius, Epistolae, a Critical Edition,* Indiana University Humanities Series 49 (Bloomington: Indiana University Press, 1962) 354-56 (for Pliny's letter) and 356-57 (for Trajan's reply). Cf. also Stout, *Scribe and Critic at Work in Pliny's Letters,* I. U. Humanities Series 30 (Bloomington: Indiana University Press, 1954); A. N. Sherwin-White, *The Letters of Pliny: A Historical and Social Commentary* (Oxford: Clarendon, 1966) 691-710, for comments on 10.96, which Morton Smith, *Jesus the Magician* (San Francisco: Harper and Row, 1978) 180, calls "a whitewash"; Ronald Syme, *Tacitus* (Oxford: Clarendon, 1963, from corrected sheets of 1st ed., 1958) 1.75-85, and 2.458-59, 633. Especially important is R. M. Grant, "Pliny and the Christians," *Harvard Theological Review* 41 (1948): 273-74, indicating parallels between Pliny's letter and Livy, *Histories,* 39.

surer of his evidence, Pliny had also questioned two female slaves under torture. He related that their testimony established what he had already learned from the renegade Christians. Pliny indicated that the two slave girls "were called *ministrae*," that is, assistants, servers, perhaps deaconesses (cf. Rom. 16:1), in any case women who had status in the Christian community and whose witness he valued as confirming what he had already discovered.

His judgement was that Christianity was a "depraved and immoderate superstition," but one which was spread throughout his province not only in the cities, but also in the villages and countryside. Justin, too, had referred to the Christian assembly as made up of city-dwellers and those of the countryside, of rich and poor alike. Pliny declared that the movement included a "multitude of people" of every age, every rank of society, and both sexes.[2] It was indeed such a massive "contagion" that by his time the pagan temples were almost desolate, pagan festivals had virtually lapsed, and it was extremely rare to find a purchaser of sacrificial animals. That last note may intimate an economic motive for his opposition to Christianity (cf. Acts 16:19; 19:24-27), but Pliny's combined references to temples, festivals, and sacrifices suggest that the real difference between Christians and their pagan fellowmen was a mode of worship.[3]

His allusions to Christian worship were exceedingly brief and tantalizing. Like Justin Martyr he gave no indication of the place.

---

[2]Smith, *Jesus the Magician*, 52, dismissed them as "innocent simpletons."

[3]M. H. Shepherd, Jr., "The Early Apologists and Christian Worship," *Journal of Religion* 18 (1938): 60-79; Jean Daniélou, *Gospel Message and Hellenistic Culture*, trans. J. A. Baker (London: Darton, Longman and Todd, 1973) 18, "The cultus was the crucial issue"; Gregory Dix, *Jew and Greek: A Study in the Primitive Church* (London: Dacre Press, 1953) 69. *Per contra*, see Nikolaus Walter, "Christusglaube und Heidnische Religiosität in Paulinischen Gemeinden," *New Testament Studies* 25 (1979): 422-42, esp. 436-41.

As a matter of fact it was liturgical practice that speeded separation of Christians from the Synagogue, namely, an addition to the Eighteen Benedictions of a curse against Jews who became Christians. Cf. G. D. Kilpatrick, *The Beginnings of the Gospel according to Saint Matthew* (Oxford: Clarendon, 1950; first published 1946) 109, 128.

Unlike Justin he made no allusion to any Christian officials. Pliny's reference to time was simply "on a particular day" (*stato die*). It is, of course, possible that it was a day decided upon at a previous meeting,[4] but the weight of opinion is that his phraseology meant Sunday, as in Justin. The hour was "before light" (*ante lucem*), that is, before dawn or daybreak, in the dark hours of early morning. He stated that Christians "were accustomed to assemble" (*essent soliti . . . convenire*), indicating a long-established practice. In the assembly at the appointed time and place the Christians proceeded to "utter" (*dicere*) mutually or alternately (*secum invicem*) a hymn or song (*carmen*) "to Christ as to a god" or "to Christ as God" (*Christo quasi deo*). Thereafter they bound themselves by solemn obligation (*sacramento*) not to commit thievery, banditry, or adultery, not to break faith nor to violate a trust when called upon for it. That was the first past of the Christian service as Pliny derived it from what he considered authentic sources.

Pliny then stated that, according to custom, the Christians "separated" or "divided" (*morem . . . discedendi*), after which they "reassembled" or "again united" (*rursusque coeundi*) for the second part of the service, namely, to "take food" (*capiendum cibum*), which Pliny declared, perhaps scornfully, to be "ordinary and harmless" (*promiscuum et innoxium*). He did not specify the interval of time between the two parts of the service. It could have been somewhat later the same day, but equally it could have been only a very short time.[5] Justin had also, without directing attention to it,

---

[4]So Samuele Bacchiocchi, *From Sabbath to Sunday* (Rome: Pontifical Gregorian University Press, 1977) 98-99. Cf. also Richard Banckham, "The Worship of Jesus in Apocalyptic Christianity," *New Testament Studies* 27 (1961): 322-41, esp. 329.

[5]Most commentators opt for a considerable lapse of time between two services: C. J. Kraemer, "Pliny and the Early Church Service: Fresh Light from an Old Source," *Classical Philology* 29 (1934): 243, 296, 299; S. L. Mohler, "The Bithynian Christians Again," ibid. 30 (1935): 169 and n. 7; D. M. Stanley, "Carmenque Christo Quasi Deo Dicere . . . , " *Catholic Biblical Quarterly* 20 (1958): 176; W. D. Maxwell, *An Outline of Christian Worship* (London: Oxford University Press, 1936) 9; Carrington, *Early Christian Church*, 1:433; Smith, *Jesus the Magician*, 53. But there is no necessity for such an interpretation.

distinguished two parts of the Christian service: the first, instructional (whether general or baptismal); the second, Eucharistic.

It may be significant that Pliny used for the assembling of the people to worship a rather solemn word, *convenire*, to come together; but for the second part of the worship, another word, *coeundi*, to unite. The latter word responds in form to the one for the break in the service, *discedendi*, which does not necessarily mean to go away, but to divide or separate. Justin indicated that the Eucharistic part was not open to everyone to participate in it, but only to baptized believers. So here Pliny may have learned about the two divisions of the service. Justin made a point of asserting that the Eucharistic food was *not* common food,[6] but Pliny probably did not trouble himself to understand the Christian conception and so referred to it as "ordinary" as well as harmless. It is quite possible that he was thereby contradicting scurrilous rumors of Christian cannibalism.

In Pliny's letter the words about the second part of Christian worship do not seem to be especially problematic, perhaps because less was revealed about it. But not so his words concerning the first part; almost every one of them bristles with questions. For example, what was the *carmen* he mentioned? The term signifies "verse as opposed to prose and the melody; it is usually restricted to lyric and epic as distinct from dramatic verse; and it may mean a religious formula or an oracular prophecy."[7] It could possibly allude to a scriptural Psalm.[8] *Christo quasi deo,* as indicated above, may mean to Christ "as to a god" or "as to God." Since they were the words of a pagan interpreting Christian language, they probably mean "as to a god," reminiscent of the Roman centurion's equally ambiguous words at Jesus' death, "Surely this man was a god's son" or "God's

---

[6] It is possible that Justin knew of Pliny's letter. At a slightly later time (ca. 150–ca. 230), Tertullian certainly knew of it; see his *Apologeticus* 2.6-10.

[7] Cabaniss, *Liturgy and Literature,* 70.

[8] Kraemer, "Pliny and the Early Church Service," 297, says it could be a Psalm, while Mohler, "The Bithynian Christians Again," 168, thought otherwise.

Son" (Mark 15:39 ‖ Matt. 27:54). But even so Pliny was aware that Christians considered their Messiah to be divine, a deity, although he himself did not do so. He was apparently aware, as were Tacitus[9] and Suetonius,[10] that Christ (Messiah) was a title, not a name. *Dicere* can mean simply to speak, say, or utter; but used with *carmen* it can mean to sing, celebrate, or speak in a solemn voice, that is, chant. Here it probably means "to chant" if *carmen* does indeed mean a Psalm. The phrase, *secum invicem,* probably means "with each other alternately."

If *carmen* means Psalm; *dicere,* to chant; and *secum invicem,* in alternating lines—what Psalm is there which could be interpreted as addressing "Christ as God" (or "a god") and could be chanted responsively? A possible New Testament *carmen Christi* is Phil. 2:6-11,[11] but it is not in such form that it could artistically be rendered "alternately." From the Old Testament, however, there is Psalm 24, which was definitely rendered "alternately" and was actually employed with reference to Messiah as "king of glory."[12] But we cannot be sure what Pliny understood or meant by his statement. If he did have reference to singing, his words would be the earliest certain evidence that the primitive Christians used music in their service. But chanting is not, in the proper sense, singing; it is a mode of reading (or reciting) with voice elevated in an emo-

---

[9]Tacitus, *Annals* 15.44.

[10]Suetonius, *Claudius* 25.4.

[11]Ralph P. Martin, *Carmen Christi* (Cambridge: University Press, 1967), a study of Phil. 2:5-11 "in recent interpretation and in the setting of early Christian worship." C. C. Coulter, "Further Notes on the Ritual of the Bithynian Christians," *Classical Philology* 35 (1940): 60-63, considered that passage "perfectly suited to antiphonal singing," but surely it is not the case. D. M. Stanley, "The Theme of the Servant of Yahweh in Primitive Christian Soteriology," *Catholic Biblical Quarterly* 16 (1954): 425, leaned slightly to it as a baptismal hymn, but recognized that it could have been Eucharistic. See B. Eckman, "A Quantitative Metrical Analysis of the Philippians Hymn," *New Testament Studies* 26 (1980): 258-66.

[12]See Cabaniss, *Liturgy and Literature,* 66-70; Mohler, "The Bithynian Christians Again," 168, denied that any Psalm was addressed to Messiah as God, but the early church certainly used some Psalms in that way.

16 • PATTERN IN EARLY CHRISTIAN WORSHIP

tional, ecstatic, or religious manner similar to, and for the same purpose as, cantillation of Scripture in the synagogue liturgy.[13] If Psalm 24 was indeed indicated, it adds to the evidence for *stato die* being Sunday, since it was the Psalm assigned for Sunday in Jewish practice.[14]

Pliny's statement has a strange antecedent in Eph. 5:19 where the writer (alluding to Col. 3:16) says, "speaking (ecstatically?) to each other with spiritual Psalms and hymns and odes" (*lalountes heautois psalmois kai humnois kai o[i]dais pneumatikois*). The Colossian statement is "singing . . . to God" (*a[i]dontes . . . to[i] theo[i]*) with spiritual Psalms, hymns, odes. There are four verbal coincidences: (1) Pliny's *carmen* is equivalent to the Ephesian (Colossian) *psalmois-humnois-o(i)dais;* (2) his *dicere* corresponds to Ephesian *lalountes* (which suggests ecstatic or heightened speech); (3) his *secum invicem* is equivalent to Ephesian *heautois;* and (4) *Christo quasi deo* is similar to Colossian *a(i)dontes . . . to(i) theo(i).*[15] The resemblances seem close enough and remarkable enough to suggest some kind of relationship. If so, the middle ground between the two statements is the Christian service of worship.

As noted above, Pliny's statement immediately following the foregoing is that at the service Christians bound themselves by solemn obligation (*sacramento*) not to commit thievery, banditry, or adultery, not to break faith nor to violate a trust (*depositum*) when called upon to return it. We note that in *sacramento* we have the word for a soldier's oath at enlistment, an affirmation of his allegiance. The figure of soldiery is a familiar New Testament expres-

---

[13]Eric Werner, *The Sacred Bridge* (New York: Columbia University Press, 1959) 103-104, on cantillation; Kraemer, "Pliny and the Early Church Service," 298. See William Beare, *Latin Verse and European Song: A Study in Accent and Rhythm* (London: Methuen, 1957) 220-22.

[14]See Cabaniss, *Liturgy and Literature,* 150 n. 19, for the evidence; also the Septuagint heading of this Psalm.

[15]Eph. 5:19-20 elaborates thus: "adontes . . . to(i) kurio(i) . . . eucharistountes . . . to(i) theo(i), that is, "singing . . . to the Lord . . . giving thanks . . . to God." See Beare, *Latin Verse and European Song,* 220.

sion for the Christian life (2 Cor. 10:3-4; Phil. 2:25; Philemon 2; 1 Tim. 1:18; 6:12; 2 Tim. 2:3; 4:7; Eph. 6:17; Rev. 19:11). Could Pliny's vague description be an account of a baptism and could this be the first appearance of the word *sacramentum* to characterize that Christian rite?[16]

It will be recalled that Justin's first account of the Christian service was of a baptism preceding the Eucharist. The oath not to commit certain crimes or vices is quite consonant with what we know of New Testament catechesis. In fact, the listing reads very much like the latter part of the Decalogue as cited in the New Testament (not to steal, commit adultery, bear false witness, or practice fraud; cf. Mark 10:19 ‖ Luke 18:20; 1 Cor. 6:9-10). It even reads like Psalm 24 and this contributes further toward identification of the *carmen* as that Psalm. The phrase, "not to deny (or violate) a trust," is reminiscent of 2 Tim. 1:12, "to guard the trust" (*paratheken, depositum;* cf. also 1 Tim. 6:20), just as the pledge not to break faith suggests 1 Pet. 5:9, an exhortation to remain steadfast in the faith. It is indeed with considerable surprise that we find the statement of a pagan governor containing so many strong allusions to Scripture.[17] Once again we remember that the middle ground between his remarks and Scripture is the Christian service of worship.

From Pliny's exposition we miss clear verbal reference to Bible reading such as we found in Justin's service, especially in the latter's second description of it. But that omission serves to remind us that the New Testament had not been codified at that early date, had probably not been completed. We find also no reference to prayers. But what we do find is an amazingly significant descrip-

---

[16]Mohler, "The Bithynian Christians Again," 167, declared, "*sacramentum* is certainly the Decalogue," but that cannot be so "certain."

[17]The possibility of Pliny's letter being inauthentic has been implied by Smith, *Jesus the Magician,* 52-53. Ernest Renan, however, deemed it improbable that a Christian forger could be able "to imitate so admirably Pliny's elegant and subtle language"; see the Renan citation in Tertullian, *Apologeticus,* trans. T. R. Glover, Loeb Classical Library (London: Heinemann, 1931) 10 n. *b;* cf. also the works by Stout indicated in n. 1 above.

tion, albeit from a pagan point of view. As in Justin, we discover Christian worship divided into two distinct segments: the first, primarily instructional; the second, "Eucharistic." Pliny's meager words are enough to reveal virtually the same general outline as in Justin. And we may, but only may, have an additional factor, unmentioned by Justin, namely, singing or music of some kind. As in the case of Justin, we find ample and clear antecedent material of biblical provenience also in Pliny, not surprising in the former, but quite astounding in the latter.

¶

Apart from Justin Martyr and Pliny the Younger, we have no other purported description of Christian worship in the second century. There were several other documents, approximately contemporary with those two authors, which present occasional indications regarding particular elements of worship. Justin was a Christian writing to pagans; Pliny was a pagan writing to a pagan; but the documents next to be considered were by Christians writing to Christians. They are Clement's (first) letter to the Corinthians, Ignatius's letters, and the *Didache*.[18]

Clement laid great stress on orderliness. "Sacrifices" and liturgies were to be at fixed seasons and hours (40:2). There were ordered ranks in the congregation: the chief celebrant (whom he called

---

[18]Martin, *Worship in the Early Church*, 2 n. 1, remarked, "These are the chief texts which contain *liturgica*." I cite reference to them internally with my own translations, using the Greek texts in Kirsopp Lake, *The Apostolic Fathers* 1, Loeb Classical Library (London: Heinemann, 1930; first published 1912). J. A. T. Robinson, *Redating the New Testament* (Philadelphia: Westminster Press, 1975) 312-35, argued for an early dating of Clement and the *Didache*, and the traditional date for Ignatius, but in a footnote (334 n. 10) mentioned his colleague, John Sturdy, who argued for a mid-second-century date for Clement and Ignatius and claimed that their writings were pseudepigraphical (Dean Sturdy kindly sent me a typescript of his paper, "Clement, Ignatius and Polycarp: A Revision of Accepted Views"). The *Didache* has been dated both early and late; on it see Richardson in Lietzmann, *Mass and Lord's Supper*, 367-406. In the case of all three documents (Clement, Ignatius, *Didache*), I adopt a ground between Robinson and Sturdy, dating them in the late first century or early second.

high priest), other priests in their proper places, "Levites" who performed their "deaconings," and lay folk according to their ordinances (40:3), or as he said a little later, "Let each of us, brothers,
in his own rank make Eucharist to God" (41:1). Clement's use of
Old Testament phraseology for the Christian orders should be
noted. He cited Isa. 6:17 about bishops and deacons to intimate that
they were not of recent establishment (42:5). Messiah's flock was
to be at peace with the presbyters set over it (54:2; 57:1). Of presbyters and their usefulness he adduced Psalm 24:1 (54:3). In chapters 59:3–61:3 he recorded a lengthy prayer which may have been
similar in content to one used in the service. All in all, however,
Clement did not add to what we can discover in Justin and Pliny,
except for his citation of Psalm 24, which may confirm our guess
that Pliny also alluded to that Psalm.

Nor does Ignatius add any specific details of the order. He confirmed Sunday ("the Lord's day"; cf. Rev. 1:10, 18) as the day of
worship (Magn. 9). He may have cited or composed a Christmas
hymn (Eph. 18-19), but did not intimate its employment in worship.[19] He did heighten the mystery of the Eucharist by characterizing it as a "drug of deathlessness, an antidote against dying" (Eph.
20:2; cf. John 6:54-58; 1 Cor. 11:29-30), and as a cult meal somewhat like a pagan sacrificial banquet, in which the worshippers "ate"
their god (Rom. 7:3; Smyrn. 7:1; Eph. 13:1; 20:2; Philad. 4).

More important for our purpose is the *Didache*. The compiler
mentioned the fast before baptism, to be engaged in by baptizer,
baptizand, and others (7:4). The Lord's Prayer was to be said thrice
daily (8:2-3), but presumably in private. Each Sunday ("the Lord's
[day] of the Lord"!) was the occasion when Christians were gathered (*sunachthentes*) to break bread and make Eucharist (14:1),
before which a reconciliation of differences was to take place (14:2),
possibly an allusion to the kiss of peace. In connection with the Eu-

---

[19]Cabaniss, *Liturgy and Literature*, 55-56; Carrington, *Early Christian Church*,
1:453; R. M. Grant, *Ignatius of Antioch*, The Apostolic Fathers: A New Translation and Commentary 4 (Camden NJ: Thomas Nelson and Sons, 1966) 49-51,
esp. 50n.

charist he quoted parts of Mal. 1:11, 14 (14:2) and no one was to participate except those who were baptized (9). Bishops and deacons, exercising the ministry of prophets and teachers, were the officers of the Eucharist (15:1).

The *Didache* gives a prayer over the Eucharistic cup and one over the broken bread (9; cf. the order of elements in Luke 22:17-19 and 1 Cor. 10:16); then a somewhat longer one afterwards (10). They seem to have been prescribed for customary occasions, since it was specified that "prophets" might make Eucharist "as they wished" (*hosa thelousin*). The third prayer concluded thus in a liturgical formula (10):

> Let grace come (cf. John 1:17)
>   and this world pass away (cf. 1 John 2:17).
> Hosanna to the God of David (Matt. 21:9, 15, Son of David)!
> If anyone is holy, let him come (Rev. 22:11, 17);
> But if not, let him repent (Rev. 3:14).
> Maranatha (1 Cor. 16:22; cf. Rev. 22:20)!
> Amen (1 Cor. 16:24).[20]

¶

It is significant and in accord with the Evangelists and Justin that Clement, Ignatius, and the *Didache* did not verbally relate the Eucharist to Messiah's death. (And, of course, Pliny did not do so.) Yet they did not explicitly associate it with the Incarnation as Justin did. With Justin and Pliny, therefore, we have all that we know unequivocally about the order or sequence of early Christian worship. With Clement, Ignatius, and the *Didache,* we have some details that help to fill in the content of the service. But with those five early documents, we have, for all intents and purposes, exhausted second-century material on the liturgy.

---

[20]J. A. T. Robinson, *Twelve New Testament Studies* (Naperville IL: Alec R. Allenson, Inc., 1962) 154-57, "The Earliest Christian Liturgical Sequence?" (a treatment of 1 Cor. 16:20-24). On the *Didache,* see also A. Verheul, "La prière eucharistique dans la Didaché," *Questions Liturgiques* 60 (1979): 197-207.

It will be logical and convenient to see what the New Testament reveals in relation to those documents. The biblical, especially New Testament, antecedents of the material in those documents have been noted above over and over again. Consequently it will not be a process of "reading into" the New Testament data the patristic outline, but using the latter quite legitimately as the goal toward which New Testament evidence leads. Before turning to the New Testament, however, it is fitting to consider the background out of which New Testament worship emerged.

CHAPTER 3

LITURGY
IN TEMPLE AND PROPHECY

ACCORDING TO THE NEW TESTAMENT the apostles and earlier disciples of the Christian movement were familiar with the Jerusalem Temple and its service.[1] For a number of years they continued their association with it even after they had professed their belief that Jesus was the promised Messiah. Jesus Himself, according to the church's record, was loyal to the Temple all His earthly life: He attended it (Mark 14:49; Matt. 26:55; Luke 21:37; 22:53) and kept its solemnities (cf. John 2:13; 4:45; 5:1; 6:4; 7:10; 10:22; 11:55; 13:29; 18:28). His zeal for it and its services was demonstrated by His cleansing the court of the Gentiles and rebuking profanation of it (Mark 11:15; Matt. 21:12; John 2:16; Luke 19:45). In His teaching He made use of illustrations derived from the Temple (Mark 14:58; Matt. 12:3-6; Luke 18:10). He condemned the Pharisees for swearing by the Temple and its altar (Matt. 23:16-21). One of His temptations is reputed to have been located on a Temple pinnacle (Matt. 4:5; Luke 4:9). It was with horror that He anticipated its ul-

---

[1]Most of this chapter is based on my article, "Liturgy-making Factors in Primitive Christianity," *Journal of Religion* 23 (1943): 43-58, esp. 43-49. See M. D. Goulder, "The Apocalypse as an Annual Cycle of Prophecies," *New Testament Studies* 27 (1981): 342-67, stressing the close relation between the liturgical reading of Ezekiel (in particular) and the Revelation.

timate destruction (Mark 13:14). Many of His declarations gain force and meaning from connection with feasts prescribed by Temple authority. It was, for example, at the Pesach season that He instituted the Eucharist and taught about His atonement (Mark 14:12-25). A later gospel suggested that it was at a feast of Succoth that He said, "I am the world's light" (John 7:2, 10, 14, 37; 8:12), and at a feast of Hanukkah that He proclaimed His unity with the Father (John 10:22-30). Jesus also inculcated respect for the lawful religious officials even if they were not of exemplary character (Matt. 23:2-5).

The early Christians were but following Jesus's footsteps when they continued affiliation with the Temple. To it they resorted for worship (Luke 24:53; Acts 2:46). The apostles kept the hours of the daily service (Acts 3:1) and even preached in the Temple area (Acts 5:20-21, 42). Although Paul was opposed to binding ordinances and requirements, he nonetheless performed Temple purifications (Acts 21:26), received a divine revelation in its precincts (Acts 22:16), and contributed to Temple use moneys he had collected (Acts 24:17-18). His thought and mind were deeply colored by the ceremonial of Temple services and he often interchanged the language of Temple and church (Rom. 12:1; 15:16; 1 Cor. 5:7; 10:1-4, 18; Phil. 4:18; Col. 2:11). According to an ancient tradition, James the Upright, foster brother of Jesus and first bishop of Jerusalem, was so in the habit of praying in the Temple courts that his knees became hardened like those of a camel.[2] And John the Evangelist is supposed to have worn the *petalon* (breastplate, ephod, turban?) of a Jewish priest.[3]

Well may we ask what was that Temple which meant so much to the mind and spirit of early Christians. The actual one which they knew was erected by Zerubbabel after return from Babylonian captivity, greatly expanded and lavishly improved by Herod. But back of that Temple was the magnificent structure that had im-

---

[2]Eusebius, *Historia ecclesiastica* 2.23.

[3]Ibid., 1.24.

mortalized the name of Solomon, king of Israel. It was described in great detail in 1 Kings 6-8 and 2 Chron. 3-7. Even further back was the tabernacle built by Moses in the wilderness according to a pattern he received on the holy mountain (Exod. 25:9). Although that tent of worship had long ago crumbled into the dust of Palestine, it continued to exercise a fascination over the thoughts and affections of pious Jews and Christians (Heb. 8:5, 9:1-5, 23).[4] The temples of Solomon, Zerubbabel, and Herod were indeed consciously modeled on the Mosaic tabernacle, with alterations necessitated by change from an impermanent, movable seat of worship to a permanent, stated one. The tent in the wilderness shone radiantly with its veils of white, blue, purple, and scarlet, while the temples glistened as the sunlight played upon walls and doors overlaid with gold and precious gems (Exod. 21:1; 2 Chron. 3:5-7).

In tabernacle and temples the furniture remained generally of the same type. In the outer court were a huge brazen laver of purification and an altar of burnt offering (Exod. 27:1-8, 30:17-21; 2 Chron. 4:1-5). Solomon's laver—so large that it was called a metallic "sea"—was five cubits high and thirty in circumference. It rested upon twelve bull-like figures and its brim was wrought like lily blossoms (2 Chron. 4:2-3, 5). In the inner court there were three golden objects: a table of presence-bread, a seven-branched candelabrum, and the altar of incense. In Solomon's Temple, because of its size, there were ten tables and ten candelabra (Exod. 25:23-40; 2 Chron. 4:7-8). The cups of the candelabra were shaped like almond blossoms (Exod. 25:33; 2 Chron. 4:21). In Zerubbabel's Temple the plan apparently called for return to the single candelabrum of the tabernacle (Zech. 4:2). The lights were to burn every night perpetually to symbolize the everlasting presence and watchfulness of God (Exod. 27:20-21; 1 Sam. 3:3; 2 Chron. 4:30).

The Holy of Holies was screened from view by a veil of white, blue, purple, and scarlet linen embroidered with figures of cherubim (Exod. 26:31-33; 2 Chron. 3:14; Matt. 27:51). Within it was

---

[4]Cf. Josephus, *Antiquities* 3.77; Philo, *Life of Moses* 3.3-14.

the ark of the covenant made of acacia wood overlaid with gold, containing the tablets of the Torah (2 Chron. 5:10; Deut. 10:2-5). According to later tradition it also contained a golden pot of manna and Aaron's budding rod (Heb. 9:4; Exod. 16:33-34; Num. 17:10). Over the ark, as a kind of covering or lid, was the mercy seat of solid gold with two cherubim (Exod. 25:17-21). In Solomon's Temple the ark and mercy seat were placed between two larger cherubim within the Holy of Holies (2 Chron. 3:10-13; 5:7-8). It was between the cherubim of the mercy seat that the Shekinah appeared and that God communicated with His people (Exod. 25:22; Num. 7:89; 1 Sam. 4:4; 2 Sam. 6:2; 2 Kings 19:15; Psalms 89:1; 99:1; Isa. 37:16). The original ark and mercy seat, used in both tabernacle and Solomon's Temple, were probably lost after the capture of Jerusalem by the Babylonians (2 Macc. 2:4-8) and were presumably replaced in the Temple of Zerubbabel and Herod by imitations.[5] The exterior of Solomon's edifice was further adorned with palm trees and chains (2 Chron. 3:5), and in front were the celebrated brass pillars, Jachin and Boaz, decorated with lilies, pomegranates, and network (2 Chron. 3:15-17; 4:12-13).

A special comment should be made about the Herodian Temple, because it was the actual one with which the first generation of Christians was familiar. It was the third one to be erected on Mount Moriah, or rather it was a rebuilding of Zerubbabel's on a larger scale more nearly to approximate the Solomonic proportions. The huge white stones, of which it was constructed, and its elevation caused it to be discernible many furlongs away. Its columns were of the ornate Corinthian order and it was curtained with veils embroidered with purple flowers. The most singular feature of the building was a golden vine (cf. John 15:1, 5) over the main entrance, with clusters of grapes the size of a man.[6] That was well known far and wide, so much so that the eminent pagan writer Plutarch supposed that the Jews were worshippers of Bacchus (Dio-

---

[5]Tacitus, *Histories* 5.9.

[6]Josephus, *Jewish Wars* 5.210; *Antiquities* 15.11.395.

nysus).[7] Tacitus reported that others thought so, too, but that he did not agree.[8] The splendor of the structure and its services is intimated by Herod's purchase of a thousand sacerdotal vestments for the ministrants at the dedication.[9]

The dress of the priests was commensurate with the magnificence of the building and its furnishings. The high priest's garments are described in full in the Bible. The first robe over the underclothes was a white checkerwork linen cassock (or alb) gathered about the waist with a cincture (Exod. 28:39). Over it was worn a blue robe, similar to a chasuble, around the skirt of which was a series of blue, purple, and scarlet pomegranates alternating with small golden bells (Exod. 28:31-34). Over that was the ephod itself, of white, blue purple, and scarlet cloth, interwoven with golden threads (Exod. 39:2-3). Two onyxes engraved with the names of the Israelitish tribes were set on the shoulders (Exod. 28:9-12). A breastplate made of the same material as the ephod, adorned with twelve precious stones, was worn on the front of the ephod, suspended from the neck by a golden chain (Exod. 28:15-28). In addition the high priest wore over his heart the mysterious Urim and Thummim (Exod. 28:30). His headdress was a turban of linen bearing a golden plate engraved with the words, "Holy to YHVH" (Exod. 28:36-37). The lesser priests apparently wore only the white cassock, cincture, and headdress without the inscribed plate (Exod. 28:40). All the clothing had symbolic significance, chiefly of intercession and atonement (Exod. 28:12, 29-30, 35, 38), but it was also for "splendor and beauty" in the service of God (Exod. 28:40). Every priest, set apart with inspiring ceremonies (Exod. 29:1-37), had his place in the special arrangement for executing the various aspects of worship (1 Chron. 24:1-19).

In tabernacle and temples worship was fixed in every detail, as a reader will discover in the book of Leviticus. There were daily,

---

[7] Plutarch, *Table Talks,* quaestio 6.

[8] Tacitus, *Histories* 5.5.

[9] Josephus, *Antiquities* 15.11.

weekly, and annual services. The use of animal blood, water, oil, and incense was profuse. Both vocal and instrumental music figured in the services and immense choirs were involved. The Psalter as it exists today was probably arranged to serve as both hymnbook and prayerbook of Zerubbabel's Temple. Some of the Psalms required several choruses and solo voices for their rendition (Psalms 24, 42-43, 107, 115); some were antiphonal (46, 136); some were responses (67—to the Aaronic blessing of Num. 6:24-26); some were processionals (120-134); some were full choirs of all voices and instruments (146-150).[10] Without going into further detail it can be seen that Temple worship was a very elaborate, moving, and dramatic liturgical service, which must have exercised an incalculable influence on primitive Christianity.

W. D. Maxwell has asserted that "the Temple worship left little mark upon Christian worship."[11] He gave several reasons for his statement: the real home of Jewish worship in Palestine was the synagogue; most Jews of the Diaspora had never seen the Temple; to Gentile converts the Temple meant little; and the Temple, destroyed in A.D. 70, was never rebuilt, while synagogues continued to exist.[12] Other scholars also attribute more influence upon the Christian movement to synagogue than to Temple. By and large that may be true, but it has been exaggerated and Temple worship has been slighted.

---

[10]R. G. Moulton, *The Modern Reader's Bible* (New York: Macmillan, 1939) 747-875; see also Mitchell Dahood, *Psalms,* 3 vols., Anchor Bible 16, 17, 17a (Garden City NY: Doubleday, 1966, 1968, 1970); Christoph Barth, *Introduction to the Psalms* (New York: Charles Scribner's Sons, 1966).

[11]Maxwell, *An Outline of Christian Worship,* 2. Maxwell's particular theory concerning Reformed liturgy, as expressed in his excellent *John Knox's Genevan Service Book 1556* (Edinburgh: Oliver and Boyd, 1931) passim and see index, "Prone," beguiled me for a number of years, but reservations have occurred to me as I intimated in "Place of the Sermon at Liturgy," *Reformed Liturgics* 4/2 (1967): 22 n. 6. There is some critique of Maxwell in H. O. Old, *The Patristic Roots of Reformed Worship* (Zurich: Theologischer Verlag, 1975) 12 n. 4; 19 nn. 2, 4; 20 and n. 2; 92 n. 1; 306 n. 3.

[12]Maxwell, *An Outline of Christian Worship,* 2.

On the contrary, Temple influence was very great—obviously so in the gospels, Acts, letter to the Hebrews, and Apocalypse; less obviously, but basically so, in the sacrificial language of Pauline literature. The whole service of the synagogue was, moreover, oriented toward the Temple: prayers were made facing Jerusalem (cf. Dan. 6:19; 1 Kings 8:48; Psalm 5:7; Jonah 2:4); the hours of worship were those of the morning and evening sacrifices in Jerusalem; and the Scripture lections kept the tabernacle and temples before the people at all times. Important also are some indications in the *Shemoneh Esreh*, parts of which were used in the synagogue from its earliest days. In older sections of those benedictions are such passages as the following which constantly reminded the congregations of the Temple service:

> O Lord our God . . . restore the service to the oracle of thy house; receive in love and favor both the fire offerings of Israel and their prayer; and may the service of thy people Israel be ever acceptable to thee. And let our eyes behold thy return in mercy to Zion. Blessed art thou, O Lord, who restorest thy divine presence unto Zion.[13]

Even that poignant prayer for forgiveness, Psalm 51, which has left its imprint on the New Testament, concludes (vss. 18-19) with an obvious reference to the Temple service: "In your good pleasure make Zion prosper; build up the walls of Jerusalem. Then there will be lawful sacrifice, whole burnt offerings to delight you; then bulls will be offered on your altar." It may, therefore, be hazarded that the services of synagogue and Temple were related; not antithetical, but complementary, the former receiving substance and meaning from the latter.

The real home of Jewish worship was thus the Temple, even if performed in the synagogue. Although Diaspora Jews may have

---

[13]As quoted in R. M. Grant, *A Historical Introduction to the New Testament* (New York: Harper and Row, 1963) 282, from the Authorized Daily Prayer Book, trans. S. Singer, 8th ed., 1915. On the Eighteen Benedictions, consult D. J. van der Sluis et al., *Elke Morgen Nieuw* (Arnhem: B. Folkertsma-Stichung voor Talmudica, 1978).

never seen the Temple, they probably (for that very reason) ideal-
ized it more than if they had seen it. That appears to be evident
from references to the tabernacle in the letter to the Hebrews (8:5;
9:1-5; 23), as well as from passages in Philo.[14] Gentile converts
would be familiar with the Temple and its liturgy from the Bible.
Although the Temple was destroyed by the Romans, the orienta-
tion of synagogue services remained the same; Scripture readings
continued to mention Temple, not synagogue; and the *Shemoneh
Esreh* still carried petition to God to restore the Temple. The influence of Temple worship was in fact formidable; it must be considered in any study of earliest Christian liturgy.

It is peculiarly interesting to ponder what a modern Jewish litur-
giologist, Eric Werner, has written about the relation of Christian
worship to Temple and synagogue. At first he asserted, like others,
that it was worship in synagogue, not Temple, which set a pattern for
the Christian church[15] and that Temple influence was only second-
hand and indirect.[16] He claimed, moreover, that "an imaginary Temple was rebuilt in the minds of Christian poets and theologians."[17] But,
in apparent contradiction, he declared, "It cannot be denied . . . that
the Temple influenced the development of Christian liturgy,"[18] that
predominance of the synagogue was not so universal as assumed.[19]
He then proceeded to show that basic prayers of Christianity, the
clerical hierarchy, and ecclesiastical calendar were derived from the
Temple.[20] Canticles, the Hallelujah, doxologies, and Psalmody were
all of Temple origin.[21] He carefully pointed out that Temple formulas
were taken up by the synagogue and "It is evident that . . . the an-

---

[14]Philo, *Life of Moses* 3.3-14.

[15]Werner, *The Sacred Bridge*, 2.

[16]Ibid., 17.   [17]Ibid., 575.   [18]Ibid., 31.   [19]Ibid., 19.   [20]Ibid., 18-20.

[21]Ibid., 138-39, 141, 169, 296, 320, etc.; see also Philip Sigal, "Early Christian and Rabbinic Liturgical Affinities: Exploring Liturgical Acculturation," *New
Testament Studies* 30 (1984): 63-90.

cient Synagogue attempted to come as near as permissible to the cult of the Temple."[22]

How strong Temple influence was can be read in Clement's letter, written about the end of the first Christian century:

> Not in every place, brothers, but only in Jerusalem are the sacrifices—daily and votive, sin and trespass—offered. Even there offering is not made in every place, but only before the shrine at the altar, after the offering has been inspected by the high priest and the aforementioned ministrants (41:2).

¶

Closely related to the actual Temple and its liturgy was the prophetic ideal as set forth by Ezekiel. During the Babylonian captivity, he described, in the form of a vision, the Temple and worship of YHVH as it should be (Ezek. 43:10-11). When the Jews returned to their homeland they tried to realize his pattern and carry it out as far as was then practicable. The basis of Ezekiel's plan was quite naturally the Mosaic tabernacle and the Solomonic Temple, but with certain differences to express more fully the separateness and holiness of YHVH (Ezek. 41:13; 43:7-9; 44:6-13). The building was to be set off more decisively from the city (Ezek. 40:20); its various courts were to be elevated (Ezek. 40:31, 34, 37, 39; 41:7; etc.); the entry gates were to be securely guarded (Ezek. 40:10, 16, etc.); certain sacrificial feasts were to be eaten in the seclusion of holy chambers (Ezek. 42:13); and no foreigners were to be allowed to perform Levitical duties in the Temple (Ezek. 44:9-11). On Solomon's Temple palm trees and chains were apparently done in bas-relief: in Ezekiel's vision there were colonnades of posts in the shape of palm trees (Ezek. 40:16, 22, etc.), and of palm trees alternating with cherubim with two faces, of a man and of a lion

---

[22]Ibid., 278-79; also A. Z. Idelsohn, *Jewish Liturgy and Its Development* (New York: Schocken Books, 1972; originally published 1932) 10-25. Cf. Sirach 50:1-21.

(Ezek. 41:18-19, etc). The latter change may have been owing to influence of heathen art surrounding the prophet.

The priestly garments are not described in as great detail as in the account of the tabernacle, but they were considered holy and were not to be worn except when the priests were ministering in the service (Ezek. 42:14; 44:19). Priests were to be clearly distinguished from laity (Ezek. 44:20-22, 25, 28-31). They were to teach as well as to sacrifice (Ezek. 44:23) and were also to be judges in controversies (Ezek. 44:24).

The services were to be daily, weekly, and annual (Ezek. 45:21, 25; 46:3, 13-15). In the law of Moses there were three annual feasts (Pesach, Shavuoth, Succoth), but in Ezekiel's vision there were only two (Pesach, Succoth; Ezek. 45:21, 25); and only one service per day in contrast to the older two (Ezek. 46:13-15). No reference was made to the ark and mercy seat nor to any of the other items in the first Temple except the altar of burnt-offering, which in Ezekiel occupied a position more important than the Holy of Holies (Ezek. 43:2-5). Another point to be observed about that ideal Temple was the stress on symmetry and proportion, so notably absent from the tabernacle and Solomon's Temple (Ezek. 40-48, passim).

A student of the Apocalypse cannot doubt that Ezekiel's vision was influential in the mind of the early church. In Rev. 21 and 22 the author's vision of the holy city, new Jerusalem, is reminiscent of Ezekiel's ideal Temple and its environs. Noteworthy are the similar descriptions of a pure stream flowing from the Temple, bordered on either bank by rows of trees for healing of the nations (Ezek. 47:1-12; Rev. 21:1-2), and the affirmation that the city shall be the very dwelling place of God (Ezek. 48:35, Rev. 22:3). Much later it was reputed to be a secret object of the medieval Templars to rebuild the Temple "on the model prophesied by Ezekiel"—a fancy illustrating the strong appeal exerted by the prophet's vision.[23]

---

[23]Albert Pike, *Morals and Dogma* (Richmond VA: L. H. Jenkins, 1930; originally published 1871) 816; A. E. Waite, *A New Encyclopedia of Freemasonry* I (New York: Weathervane Books, 1970) 422.

CHAPTER 4

LITURGY
CELESTIAL AND PAGAN[1]

CONSIDERATION OF EZEKIEL'S PROPHETIC VISION of the Temple as
it should be is closely connected with a concept of worship as it is
in heaven in God's presence. There is a well-known passage, Isa.
6:1-5, which deals with that subject. It is a vision seen by the
prophet "in the year that King Uzziah died" when God appeared
to him, seated on an exalted throne. Around Him were six-winged
seraphim chanting, "Holy, holy, holy is YHVH almighty; the whole
earth is full of His splendor." Before Him was an altar with fire upon
it. The doorposts and threshold shook at the sound of the angelic
choir and the Temple was filled with smoke (of the sacrifice or of
God's presence). For a brief moment the prophet may have peered
into the very presence of God, but the seraphs referred signifi-
cantly to God's radiant glory on earth. With slight amplification their
Sanctus hymn is still employed in Christian worship (cf. Rev. 4:8).

The Isaianic verses are the most notable Old Testament mention of celestial worship, but there are other brief allusions. In Job
38:7 are the reputed words of God that before creation of the earth

---

[1]Like the preceding chapter, this one relies on my article, "Liturgy-making
Factors in Primitive Christianity." See also Goulder, "The Apocalypse as an Annual Cycle of Prophecies."

"the morning stars sang together and all God's sons [angels?] shouted for joy." In Solomon's prayer at the Temple dedication the king acknowledged that his structure could hardly contain God if the highest heavens were incapable of doing so (2 Chron. 6:18). The Psalmist called upon angels, all the heavenly host, the highest heavens to praise YHVH (Ps. 148:2, 4) in His celestial sanctuary, even to sing His praise with the awesome word *Hallelujah* (Ps. 150:1, and elsewhere).[2] That concept passed into one of cosmic worship, so beloved of the church fathers (cf. *Did.* 14:3; Justin, *Dial.* 41), in a statement that God's name is (or will be) great among the nations from east to west (or from dawn to dusk) and that incense and pure sacrifices are (or will be) offered to Him everywhere (Mal. 1:11; cf. Phil. 2:10).

There should be no wonder that New Testament writers conceived of supernal worship as being the reality of which terrestrial worship was a copy and shadow (Heb. 8:5). Earthly worship should be patterned according to the heavenly model (Exod. 25:40), because what is done on earth is but an imperfect imitation of heavenly and perfect worship (Heb. 8:1-6; 9:11, 23; 10:1). The center of celestial liturgy, as should be the center of the earthly, is Jesus (Heb. 12:22-24; Eph. 1:20-21; 2:6-7), who mediates between the two worships (John 1:51; Heb. 4:14).

Large sections of the last book of the New Testament purport to be descriptions of worship in heaven.[3] The visions took place on "the Lord's day" (Rev. 1:10), traditionally a Sunday (cf. Rev. 1:18,

---

[2]Cf. Cabaniss, *Liturgy and Literature*, 114-21. (Note 4 on p. 168 was written by my editors, not by me, and the additional note on p. 164 also is attributable to them.)

[3]Ibid., 42-52. J. Massyngberde Ford, *Revelation*, Anchor Bible 38 (Garden City NY: Doubleday, 1975), denied the Christian interpretation of the book, relating it rather to John the Baptizer. Robinson, *Redating the New Testament*, 225, observed that Ford's commentary was "eccentric." See A. A. Bell, "The Date of John's Apocalypse," *New Testament Studies* 25 (1978): 93-102, placing it about A.D. 68-69; Otto Böcher, "Johanneisches in der Apokalypse des Johannes," *New Testament Studies* 27 (1981): 310-21, esp. 318, placing it between A.D. 90 and 100.

an allusion to the Lord's resurrection),[4] the time of earthly worship. The writer's first glimpse was of the Lord, "One like a son of man," clothed in a long vestment with golden cincture, standing in the midst of seven golden lampstands, with seven stars in His hand (Rev. 1:13-16). After a while the seer was transported to heaven. There he saw One seated on a throne and around the throne a rainbow. On either side were twelve other thrones occupied by crowned presbyters. In front of them were seven lighted candles and a great laver (here called a "glassy sea"; cf. 2 Chron. 4:2), also an altar (Rev. 6:9). At the corners of the main throne, or perhaps supporting it, were four creatures (similar to those of Ezek. 1:5-14 and to the seraphim of Isa. 6:2), singing ceaselessly both night and day a version of the *Sanctus* (Rev. 4:2-8). The twenty-four presbyters removed their crowns and prostrated themselves in adoration (Rev. 4:9-10). Then appeared a Lamb, once slain, who took the scroll with seven seals from the right hand of the One on the throne. The four creatures and the twenty-four presbyters thereupon again fell down, this time before the Lamb, singing praises accompanied by music on harps, as billowing incense (identified as prayers of the saint, Rev. 5:8) arose. Suddenly their song was joined by the voices of myriads of angels and of every creature in heaven, on earth, under the earth, and in the sea (Rev. 5:6-13). The praise was punctuated with the solemn *Amen* (Rev. 5:14). As the scene expanded it took in a countless multitude of martyrs (cf. Rev. 6:9, 11) from every land, clothed in white garments and carrying palm branches (reminiscent of the feast of Shavuoth). They added their voices to the praise, including repetition of the *Amen* (Rev. 7:9-14; cf. 15:2-4).

Somewhat later God's Temple in heaven was opened and the ark of the covenant, lost since the Babylonian captivity, was revealed (Rev. 11:19; cf. 15:5). Following that the writer saw a sun-clothed, moon-borne, star-crowned woman who brought forth a male Child destined to rule all nations (Rev. 12:1-2, 5; cf. 19:15). Satan attempted to harm the Child and mother, but he was cast out

---

[4]Per contra, Bacchiocchi, *From Sabbath to Sunday*, 111-23.

upon earth where he waged war upon Messiah's followers. Perhaps most striking of all is the scene in chapter 19 where great multitudes in heaven sang *Hallelujah* (Rev. 19:1, 3-4, 6), the antiphon on many of the Old Testament Psalms, a word with incredible influence upon Christian liturgy.[5] The Lamb thereafter appeared as a conquering warrior bearing the names "The Word of God" and "King of kings and Lord of lords" (Rev. 19:13, 16). After His appearance ensued the ultimate destruction of Satan, death, and Hades (Rev. 20:10, 14). The conclusion of the book is a picture of a new heaven and a new earth, with new Jerusalem as the bride of Messiah (Rev. 21:1-2). No temple was in the city except God and the Lamb (Rev. 21:22). From their throne flowed through the city "a river of the water of life" (Rev. 22:1-2). And Messiah's servants will worship Him and reign for ever and ever (Rev. 22:3-5) with Him, who is Alpha and Omega, the root and offspring of David, the bright morning star (Rev. 22:13, 16).

¶

Jewish worship, a prophetic ideal of worship, and a concept of worship in heaven might have impinged upon the minds of those earliest Christians who were of Jewish origin. Even more so perhaps did they fill the minds of that "large number of priests" who were reputed to have accepted the Christian faith (Acts 6:7). As noted earlier, James the Upright, foster brother of Jesus, and John, one of His earliest adherents, both had, according to church tradition, some intimate association with the priesthood of Israel. The Baptizer John, Jesus's predecessor, was of priestly extraction on both paternal and maternal lines (Luke 1:5).

In addition to traditional Jewish worship, we should note the possibility of influence of converts from sectarian sources. The Essenes, for instance, strict Mosaists except for their objection to animal sacrifice, practiced their cultus on the shores of the Dead Sea

---

[5]Cf. Cabaniss, *Liturgy and Literature,* 114-21.

facing the rising sun instead of Jerusalem.[6] Philo, a contemporary of Paul, described a group known as Therapeutae, concentrated in Egypt but also scattered throughout the Greco-Roman world. They were of Jewish origin, an ascetic community devoted to Scripture. Philo mentioned their all-night vigils, hymns, and organization. The portrayal of their use of hymnody is especially important: a soloist sang the text and the rest joined only in the refrain.[7]

¶

But there were long-standing pagan influences even on the religion of Israel and its worship.[8] The prophet Jeremiah spoke of incense and libations offered by Hebrews to the "queen of heaven" (Jer. 44:17-25), probably the goddess Astarte. Ezekiel had presumably seen women at the Temple door lamenting the god Tammuz (Adonis) and men within the Temple turning their backs to the holy place and worshipping the rising sun (Ezek. 8:14-16). Stephen, in his address, cited Amos 5:26 with reference to Hebrews venerating the gods Moloch and Rephan (Acts 7:43). Despite all efforts by prophets and periodic reformers, there remained a substratum of pagan influence embedded in the generally stalwart monotheistic religion of the Jews (cf. 1 Kings 11:4-8).

Very soon in the life of the early church converts came directly from paganism without the purging effect of Judaism. Paul alludes to them in the earliest book of the New Testament, Gal. 4:9, when he speaks of his converts in Asia Minor as "formerly . . . in bondage to beings that by nature are no gods" and of those beings as "weak

---

[6]Josephus, *Jewish Wars* 2.8.2-13.

[7]Eusebius, *Historia ecclesiastica* 2.17.3-24.

[8]See G. Widengren, "Early Hebrew Myths and Their Interpretation," in S. H. Hooke, ed., *Myth, Ritual, and Kingship* (Oxford: Clarendon, 1960), 149-203; H. H. Rowley, "Ritual and the Hebrew Prophets," in ibid., 236-60; S. G. F. Brandon, "The Myth and Ritual Position Critically Considered," ibid., 261-91, esp. 279-84 (for the New Testament); Smith, *Jesus the Magician*, 101; D. Flusser, "Paganism in Palestine," in S. Safrai and M. Stern, eds., *The Jewish People in the First Century* (Philadelphia: Fortress, 1976), 1069-79.

and beggarly elemental spirits." Somewhat later he exhorted the Colossians not to let anyone delude them concerning worship of angels. Such a person, he wrote, was an apostate—indicating by the very epithet that the person practicing that worship purported to be a Christian (Col. 2:16-19; cf. 1 Pet. 1:18).

It was inevitable that strains of the old paganism would affect nascent Christianity. Paul mentions that possibility in Gal. 4:10-11 in terms that suggest an influence on worship, "You are observing days and months, seasons and years," he wrote, "I fear that I have wasted my efforts on you." In light of the context his opposition was not to Judaic ceremonies (which Paul himself continued to keep, 1 Cor. 5:8; 16:8; cf. Acts 18:4, 21; 27:19), but to pagan festivals which may, of course, have been adopted by some Jewish or Jewish-Christian groups. One of the most remarkable evidences of a degree of pagan influence in terms of worship comes from an unguarded description which Paul gave of himself in one of his later writings, Rom. 15:16. There the apostle depicts himself as a "liturgical ministrant" proclaiming the gospel "as a priestly functionary" poised to "offer" Gentiles to the Lord as a "ritually purified sacrifice." The language could have been Hebraic, but it was more likely pagan in its implication. As indicated, both Paul and Justin Martyr suggested that the Christian Eucharist was in some way comparable with pagan worship.

¶

Of details in the worship of paganism coeval with emerging Christianity, we are at a loss. Even Christian writers who had been initiated into some of the mystery religions were reluctant to reveal the secrets. As late as the second half of the second century Justin remarked to his hearers that of the rites of Mithraism "you either know or can learn" (*Apol.*, 66). And his student, Tatian, both church father and heretic, was indeed a member of several mysteries before his conversion to Christianity (*Ad Graecos* 29). But we are not left in doubt about the effect of those impressive rites.

In the *Metamorphoses* (*Golden Ass*) of Apuleius,[9] a pagan contemporary of Justin Martyr, there are two sketches of the public worship of Egyptian Isis in Rome. Lucius, the protagonist of the story, addressed her as "queen of heaven" and identified her with Ceres of Eleusis, Venus of Paphos, Diana of Ephesus (cf. Acts 19:21-28, 34), and Proserpina (11.2). In the vision the goddess herself accepted the titles of the Great Mother adored by the Phrygians, Cecropian Minerva of Athens, Paphian Venus of Cyprus, Diana Dictynna of Crete, Juno, Bellona, Hecate, Rhamnusian Nemesis, and Queen Isis (11.4).

One of Apuleius's sketches pictures a scribe of the goddess sitting in an elevated place reading from a book, then offering prayer for the good fortune of prince, senate, the equestrian order, all the Roman people, and sailors and ships. Apparently he spoke in Latin, for at the end it is noted with special emphasis that he announced the dismissal in Greek, "*laios aphesis*" (11.17).[10] That was for a special occasion. On an ordinary day, very early in the morning,[11] a priest drew aside the curtains of the shrine to reveal a statue of the goddess. Thereafter he prepared the "divine thing" (*rem divinam*) on various altars with supplications (litanies?) and drew water for the libation. Others joined him in singing salutations to the dawn, thus proclaiming the first hour of the day (11.20).

The initiation of Lucius into the mysteries began with purification by water, followed by the imparting of certain secrets and his being clothed with a new linen garment. It was at that stage that Apuleius had Lucius declare:

> I approached the confines of death. I trod the gate of Proserpina.
> I was borne through all the elements. Now I have returned. At
> midnight I saw the sun gleaming with bright light. I came before

---

[9]I have used the Latin text of the Loeb Classical Library edition (London: Heinemann, 1919; first published 1915). Translations are my own and I have made internal references to the work of Apuleius.

[10]The Greek is garbled and it may be read otherwise.

[11]Cf. Pliny's *ante lucem.*

> gods below and gods above. I worshipped them near at hand. Al-
> though you have heard what I have related, you must conceal it,
> for I have told you only what can be revealed without offending
> the understanding of the profane (11.23).

Feasting followed emergence from that ceremony of initiation.

Apuleius had reference only to the religion of Isis, but there was considerable interchange of ceremonies in accord with the syncretistic character of the mystery initiations.[12] We will recall that it was specifically a Mithraic rite with which Justin Martyr compared the Christian Eucharist. Yet the similarity of the two Isiac sketches above and the two chapters in Justin are remarkable.

¶

Worship in state or civil paganism of the Roman world was public. Pagans were quite aware that the traditional pantheon was more a poetic device than a reality, yet they believed that maintenance of the old cultus was somehow beneficial to the state and must be perpetuated. Even after the success of Christianity, it survived in attenuated form in the Roman Senate, as the affair of the altar of Victory in the latter years of the fourth century indicated. Although the statue of Victory had been a part of the Senate building since the reign of Augustus, it was removed by Gratian (emperor, 315-383). After the latter's death the Senate petitioned for its restoration. But the days of the old official paganism were over. G. G. Coulton has beautifully suggested the dignity and appeal of that paganism which caused it to last so long. He asked for what reason should a Roman citizen "leave the marble temples, the accumulated statues and paintings of all the centuries, the stately ceremonial, the white-robed priests and the incense, the grave

---

[12]See, e.g., S. Angus, *The Mystery-Religions and Christianity* (New York: Scribners's, 1925); H. R. Willoughby, *Pagan Regeneration* (Chicago: University of Chicago Press, 1929). See now G. D'Alviella, *The Mysteries of Eleusis. The Secret Rites and Rituals of the Classical Greek Mystery Traditions* (Wellingborough UK: Aquarian Press, 1981).

honorable well-born men and women, thronging the sanctuary?
Why leave these people, whose mere conformity with the ancient
ritual, however superficial or careless, grouped them around the
daily sacrifices into a picture more impressive than any on the walls
of the temple itself? For," he continued, "though modern writers
may claim that the Roman Mass-ritual is 'art at full tide,' yet Pagan
worship, under that Southern sun, must have been . . . pictur-
esque."[13]

For what reason indeed should or would a Roman citizen abandon such ancestral worship—unless for another worship equally, if
not more, impressive? As mentioned earlier, Pliny had already implied as much and Justin, too, may be similarly understood. Over
forty years ago M. H. Shepherd, Jr., showed that it was just such
disparity of cult which evoked governmental opposition to Christianity and, to some extent, the disdain of segments of Mediterra-
nean society.[14] Thus it was that Christian apologists, of whom Justin
was one of the earliest, had to defend the Christian cultus against
both genuine misunderstanding and malicious gossip, a subject on
which Pliny also may have ventured his opinion.

¶

Early Christians, or at least their leaders, thought and wor-
shipped in an ambience which grew out of Jewish worship, fore-
most as known in the Temple, but also as in the synagogue which
reflected practice in the Temple. It was borne in upon them not only
from actual participation but also from their familiarity with the
Torah. It was illuminated by prophetic descriptions of an ideal
Temple and its worship. It was brightened and intensified by what
they conceived as the eternal worship in heaven in God's very

[13]G. G. Coulton, *Medieval Panorama* (Cambridge: University Press, 1939)
14-15.

[14]Shepherd, "The Early Apologists and Christian Worship," 60-79.

presence. Of that, earthly worship could only be a dim reflection. But somewhere in neglected areas of their mind lurked ideas of pagan worship, either as filtered through Judaism or as experienced by some of their fellows. We may now try to penetrate what the New Testament contains about Christian worship or, to employ the technical term, Christian liturgy.

CHAPTER 5

THE NEW TESTAMENT EVIDENCE OF LITURGY

FOR ALMOST TWO DECADES AFTER THE CRUCIFIXION the Christian church existed, even flourished, without any Christian literature, that is, without any that has survived except as incorporated in later literature. But the church did continue and grow. It had its faithful members, the ministry of apostles, missionaries, and teachers, its services of worship, the sacraments, its creative impulse leading to Christian forms of expression.[1] It had the Old Testament so far as then assembled or selections from it. Above all, it had the "living voice" of persons who had seen and heard Jesus, and of their immediate converts whom they had carefully instructed in the Faith. Perhaps the most significant of the latter persons was Paul, who became the first to compile a Christian literature out of what he had learned from his teachers.[2]

---

[1]Cf. Walter Pater, *Marius the Epicurean* (London: Macmillan, 1924), 277, "The wonderful liturgical spirit of the church, her wholly unparalleled genius for worship. . . . " The passage occurs near the end of ch. 22.

[2]M. S. Enslin, *The Literature of the Christian Movement,* Part III of *Christian Beginnings,* Harper Torchlight Edition (New York: Harper and Brothers, 1956; first published 1938) 205-206; R. M. Grant, *Historical Introduction to the New Testament* (New York: Harper and Row, 1963) 176; Samuel Sandmel, *A Jewish Understanding of the New Testament* (Cincinnati: Hebrew Union College Press, 1956) 39, etc. Robinson, *Redating the New Testament* 352, of course, dissented.

Not only was it natural, therefore, for the incipient New Testament to reflect the worship of early Christianity, but in a sense the New Testament was, whatever else, a liturgical book. Its contents were written to be read publicly "in church." Clearly stated in several instances (cf. 1 Thess. 5:27; Col. 4:16; perhaps John 20:31; Mark 13:14; 1 Tim. 4:13; Rev. 1:3; 22:18), it is evident in the solemn beginnings and conclusions of so many of Paul's letters. Certain whole books seem very early to have been used in liturgical fashion, either as lectionaries or to accompany lectionary readings. That has been amply suggested of the gospels of Mark, Matthew, Luke, and John.[3] Peter's first letter has been explicated as a baptismal liturgy or homily at a baptism.[4] Archbishop Carrington intimated that 1 Corinthians was a Paschal letter and 2 Corinthians a Pentecostal letter; also that the letter to the Hebrews might have been a Christian *megillah* for Yom Kippur.[5] The letter of James can be analyzed as an episcopal homily, addressing in turn the serried ranks of an early Christian congregation assembled for worship.[6] M. H. Shepherd, Jr., has argued that the Apocalypse received its particular organization in terms of the structure of the

---

[3]Philip Carrington, *The Primitive Christian Calendar. I. Introduction and Text* (Cambridge: University Press, 1952) and *According to Mark;* G. D. Kilpatrick, *The Origins of the Gospel According to St. Matthew;* M. D. Goulder, *The Evangelists' Calendar, A Lectionary Explanation of the Development of Scripture* (London: SPCK, 1978); Aileen Guilding, *The Fourth Gospel and Jewish Worship* (Oxford: Clarendon, 1960). On Mark in particular see my *Liturgy and Literature,* 37-41, and P. B. Lewis, "Indications of a Liturgical Source in the Gospel of Mark," *Encounter* 39 (1978): 385-94. See now E. Trocmé, *The Passion as Liturgy. A Study in the Origin of the Passion Narratives in the Four Gospels* (London: SCM, 1983). About twenty-five years ago at some unremembered place and from a forgotten person, I overheard an amusing characterization of all this as a "quest for the *liturgical* Jesus"!

[4]F. L. Cross, *I Peter: A Paschal Liturgy* (London: Mowbray, 1954). Per contra, E. G. Selwyn, *The First Epistle of St. Peter,* 2nd ed. (London: Macmillan, 1958).

[5]Carrington, *Primitive Christian Calendar* 1:42-44.

[6]Allen Cabaniss, "A Note on Jacob's Homily," *Evangelical Quarterly* 47 (1975) 219-22.

Easter vigil.[7] The author of 2 Pet. 3:6 confirmed Paul's own statement that the Pauline letters were read aloud. Although that assertion does not specifically identify their use in the church service, it does identify them as "Scripture," perhaps implying their use in the liturgy.

The primitive Christian church also continued the Jewish practice of reading "the law and the prophets." That seems to be evident from the use of extensive passages from the Old Testament in the books of Acts and Hebrews, but also elsewhere (cf. Rom. 1:2-4; 16:26; 1 Tim. 4:13). Such reading was supplemented by a peculiarly Christian interpretation (Luke 4:20-21; 1 Tim. 4:13; Acts 13:14-43; 1 Cor. 15:3-7; Rom. 1:2-4). All this signifies that "Scripture" in the earliest Christian church meant the Old Testament, especially the Torah and the prophets. As noted above, 2 Pet. 3:16 is the only New Testament allusion to any part of the New Testament as "Scripture." But the whole New Testament is so full of Old Testament citations and allusions as to prove the point that the Old Testament was the Scripture of the early church, an inheritance from Judaism.[8]

As late as the days of Ignatius of Antioch, when some gospels were probably in existence, there were still Christians who claimed that if it was not in the "archives" (Old Testament?), they would not believe the gospel (Philad. 8:2).[9] Ignatius himself, although presumably aware of some New Testament writings, seemed to express preference for the "living voice" rather than something written, that is, for the oral tradition (ibid.).[10] Paul, too, referred not only

---

[7]M. H. Shepherd, Jr., *The Paschal Liturgy and the Apocalypse* (Richmond VA: John Knox Press, 1960): Goulder, "The Apocalypse as an Annual Cycle of Prophecies."

[8]E. C. Blackman, *Marcion and His Influence* (London: SPCK, 1948). On Marcion see M. S. Enslin, "The Pontic Mouse," *Anglican Theological Review* 27 (1945): 1-16.

[9]See W. R. Schoedel, "Ignatius and the Archives," *Harvard Theological Review* 71 (1978): 97-106.

[10]Cf. the statement attributed to Papias in Eusebius, *Historia ecclesiastica* 3.39.4.

to the Old Testament in his teaching, but also to the oral tradition (1 Cor. 15:3-6; cf. 11:23). Consequently we can look to the New Testament not only for evidence that parts of the Old Testament and some of Paul's letters were read in the early Christian liturgy, but also for the fact that some kind of interpretation, exposition, or exhortation accompanied the reading (1 Tim. 4:13).

Prayer was characteristic of early worship. Supplications, prayers, petitions, and thanksgivings are specially mentioned as offered for all persons (1 Tim. 2:1-2). The word *Amen* was spoken in connection with prayers, sometimes spontaneously (1 Cor. 14:16), but more generally as a common response after a formulaic conclusion (2 Cor. 1:20). So closely was that affirmatory word identified with some allusion to Jesus that He Himself was designated by it as a title (Rev. 3:14). The "Lord's Prayer" was employed both as a model (Matt. 6:9-13) and as a form of prayer (Luke 11:2-4). It has been aptly suggested that the word *Abba* (father) in Gal. 4:6 and Rom. 8:15 was a mnemonic for the Lord's Prayer.[11] It is also possible what the words *Maranatha* (1 Cor. 16:20; *Did.* 10:6; cf. Rev. 22:20) are the oldest of all Christian prayers, used for many decades in the original Aramaic and indeed, according to the *Didache* (10:6), in a Eucharistic context.[12]

Under the rubric, "the breaking of (the) bread," we find also that the Eucharist was celebrated on a weekly basis, perhaps at first on a daily basis (daily, Acts 2:45; 5:42; weekly, Acts 20:7). Paul is our first witness that it was a primary feature of worship, to be carried out with frequency (1 Cor. 11:26), not annually like the Pesach. At first it was probably in small groups in private houses, but later, as the church grew, in more spacious houses that could accommodate

[11]Oscar Cullmann, *Early Christian Worship*, 13 and n. 2; cf., however, Morton Smith, "Pauline Worship as Seen by Pagans," *Harvard Theological Review* 73 (1980): 247 and n. 22, where the word is implicitly called ecstatic "jabberwocky" and compared with "*hubbahubba* and the like in modern popular songs."

[12]See Hans Lietzmann, *Messe und Herrenmahl*, 3rd ed. (Berlin: Walter de Gruyter, 1955; originally published 1926) 237; Cullmann, *Early Christian Worship*, 20; Robinson, *Twelve New Testament Studies*, 154-57.

the larger numbers (1 Cor. 11:22), that is, in houses of well-to-do members (Philem. 2, 22). The Eucharistic part, as distinguished from the instructional part, was perhaps preceded by some kind of expression of reconciliation (1 Cor. 11:25-26; James 5:16; cf. Matt. 5:23-24) which was acknowledged in the "kiss of peace" as mentioned by Justin. Thus far, then, the sequence of early Christian liturgy was scriptural lections, homily, prayers, and the Eucharist, just as we observed in Justin about a century later.[13]

The New Testament gives only slight intimations of the structure of worship, but they are of some importance. The first is, of course, from Paul. In Rom. 10:14 there is a series of questions summarized thus: How can they pray unless they have believed? How can they believe unless they have heard? How can they hear without an interpreter? In Rom. 10:17 occurs the statement that belief comes from hearing the message and the message derives from Messiah's word. Arranged in chronological order these verses give us this sequence: the Lord's word, its interpretation, its acceptance, and prayer. To this we can add Paul's exhortation in Phil. 4:6, translated thus: "Let your requests be made known to God by prayer and supplication with Eucharist." In Acts 2:42 we find this sequence: the teaching of the apostles and fellowship with them, the "breaking of the bread," and the prayers. That is virtually the same as with Paul—hearing and acceptance, Eucharist and prayers. It is evident from the New Testament, although nowhere explicitly stated, that only professed believers, the baptized, could share in the Eucharist,[14] for baptism was the mode of initiation into the company of the faithful.

To this point what we have extracted from the New Testament about Christian worship might be deemed somewhat drab, color-

---

[13]Cf. R. Moloney, "The Early Eucharist: An Hypothesis of Development," *Irish Theological Quarterly* 45 (1978): 167-76; also his "The Early Eucharist: the Jewish Background," *Milltown Studies 2 (1978): 1-10*.

[14]Per contra, N. M. Pritchard, "Profession of Faith and Admission to Communion in the Light of 1 Corinthians 11 and other Passages," *Scottish Journal of Theology* 33 (1980): 55-70, suggests the presence of unbelievers at the primitive Eucharist.

less, and austere. But we must now turn to elements of the "numinous," of awe, that surrounded by it. The mystery of the sacraments, baptism and Eucharist, will be treated separately in the next chapter. Here, however, we shall note certain other elements which lent color and appeal to the early liturgy.

(1) The first note is that of intimacy. The mere fact of meeting in a house would tend to induce such a feeling (Acts 2:46; 5:42; 20:7-11; Philem. 2). In the circumstances the compact congregation might indeed feel that it was God's true Israel (Gal. 6:16; Phil. 2:3); that no power— celestial, terrestrial, or infernal—could destroy it (Rom. 8:38-39; Eph. 6:12; cf. Matt. 16:18); that it was God's true Temple (1 Cor. 3:16); that it was composed of citizens of heaven (2 Cor. 3:20); that their worship was a spiritual sacrifice (Rom. 12:1; Heb. 13:15); that their real altar was in heaven (Heb. 12:22-24; 13:10; Eph. 3:10; Rev. 6:9; 16:7); that angels were present at their worship (1 Cor. 11:10); that heavenly worship and theirs coincided (cf. Matt. 6:10); that the Shekinah, symbol of God's presence, was among them (James 2:1, Greek; Matt. 18:20); that the church was the bride of Messiah (2 Cor. 11:2) and a second Eve (2 Cor. 11:3).

(2) Another note was an intense awareness of the presence and activity of the Holy Spirit which sometimes expressed itself in ecstatic utterance called "speaking in tongues" (1 Cor. 12:7-11). That manifestation may have been ejaculations of the Hebrew words *Amen, Hallelujah,* perhaps *Hosanna* (Mark 11:9-10; Matt. 21:9, 15; John 12:13; *Did.* 10:6), which would not be the everyday Aramaic speech of Palestinian Christians. In Greek-speaking areas Aramaic words like *Maranatha* were probably added (1 Cor. 16:22). Another manifestation was called "prophecy" (1 Cor. 14:3, 5, 24), which was probably an exhortation or Christian interpretation based on the scriptural lections (1 Cor. 14:6; 29-30, 31-32; Rom. 12:6). Such utterances, although lasting into the second century, were already looked upon in the New Testament as tending to be disorderly (1 Cor. 14:33; 39-40) and as requiring to be severely tested and even restrained (1 Cor. 13:8; 14:2-19; 1 John 4:1-2; etc.). Even

though not forbidden, they must be employed for the strengthening of the church (1 Cor. 14:26).[15]

(3) At this early date, moreover, as certainly at a later period, the members of the Christian assembly may have felt another peculiar intensity during their gathering for worship. There was a possibility that such a meeting might be suspect by outsiders. At the beginning there was no particular danger of physical persecution, but there was always the chance of misdirected gossip, questioning, criticism, and resentment. Later there would be a real peril of arrest, arraignment, and death. It is significant that Justin Martyr, in his examination before a Roman prefect, deliberately hedged when asked where the Christians met.[16]

(4) Lastly, still another note of warmth in the early Christian liturgy may have been added by the use of Psalms, hymns, and canticles (Col. 3:16; Eph. 4:19). The Temple employed the Psalms.[17] They were sung by trained choirs, often accompanied by many musical instruments (1 Chron. 23:5; 25:1; 2 Chron. 7:6; 29:30; 35:12). That practice of singing with choirs and instruments was definitely conceived of as characterizing worship in heaven (cf. Rev., passim). There were also hymns and canticles, modeled largely on the Psalms (cf. Rev., passim; Phil. 2:5-11; Eph. 5:14; 1 Tim. 3:16; Col. 1:13-20; 1 Pet. 1:3-5; perhaps John 1:1-18 in part).

One wonders how first-century Christians managed to *sing* prose Psalms, hymns, and canticles without trained choirs and musical instruments. There is a possibility that a solo voice sang the verses and the congregation joined in simple responses such as *Amen* and *Hallelujah,* or as in Psalm 136, "His mercy lasts for ever." It could also be that the so-called singing was in reality intoning or chanting on a small range of notes. We recall that, strictly speaking, intoning or chanting is simply heightened *speech,* following the rise and fall of accented syllables. But even so, there is another question: how

---

[15]For a totally different picture, see M. Smith, "Pauline Worship," 241-49.

[16]Quoted from *Acta Justini* 3, in Dix, *The Shape of the Liturgy,* 20.

[17]Werner, *Sacred Bridge,* 320; later taken up by the synagogue.

could that be if most of the people were only semiliterate or if there were not enough written copies for everyone? A possible answer may be that the Psalms, hymns, and canticles were memorized. Another answer may be that such "singing" or chanting was a spontaneous performance by individual persons. The latter seems to be the implication of James 5:13, "If any *one* is happy, let him sing a Psalm"; of 1 Cor. 14:26, "when you [plural] come together, each *one* has a Psalm"; of Col. 3:16, "teaching and admonishing *each other* with Psalms, hymns, and spiritual canticles"; of Eph. 5:19, "uttering to *each other* in Psalms and hymns and spiritual canticles."

A third answer to the question posed above could be that in the church service as such there was no singing.[18] The undoubted hymn in Eph. 5:14 is introduced by the phrase, "Wherefore it *says*" (*legei*, not even *lalei*). Almost a century later there was no reference to singing in Justin Martyr's service, as we have already observed. It is true that Pliny mentioned *carmen . . . dicere*, but, as we have seen, that phrase probably means the elevated *speaking* voice as in chanting. None of the various references given above to so-called hymns places them in a context of Christian liturgy. In Paul's various lists of "gifts" among church members, he does not allude to singers (1 Cor. 12:4-10; 12:28-30; 13:1-3; Rom. 12:6-8). The bare mention of a hymn in 1 Cor. 14:26 is left unelaborated, as instruction, revelation, tongues, and interpretation are not (on instruction or prophecy, 1 Cor. 12:29, 31; on revelation, 14:30; on tongues, 14:27; on interpretation, 14:28).

That singing of some kind was featured among early Christians is abundantly indicated, but it must have been done apart from the liturgy, as we see when Paul and Silas sang at midnight in a Philippian jail (Acts 16:25). It seems that such singing as was done in the primitive church was for the sake of instruction, as in the case of Paul and Silas just cited. It appears also in Col. 3:16 and Eph. 5:19 (see above), as well as in the close association of singing and

---

[18]Ibid., 501, 550.

instruction in 1 Cor. 14:26. The foregoing consideration leads to the point that it may have been baptismal utterance rather than Eucharistic (possibly intimated by Pliny), and that it was definitely antiphonal, perhaps between ministrant and catechumens. It may, therefore, have been credal, "a formula of sound words" (2 Tim. 1:13) memorized for doctrinal content, hence instructional. It is certainly to be recognized that the so-called hymns in the New Testament are profoundly theological. It is worth stressing that the book (the Apocalypse) that contains so many canticles, hymns, and fragments of Psalms was anciently ascribed to that John called "the theologian." Other credal expressions not already alluded to are 1 Cor. 12:3 (the simplest), Col. 2:9-15, James 2:19 (possibly the Shema).

Although early Christian missionaries took advantage of the synagogue Sabbath services (cf. Acts 13:14f.; 16:13; 17:2; 18:4), it appears that Jerusalem Christians attended the daily services of the Temple (Acts 2:46; 5:12, 42), following that with their own distinctive gatherings in their homes, at first daily but ultimately on a weekly basis. It was apparently the weekly practice that prevailed in the Diaspora (Acts 20:7; 1 Cor. 16:1; Rev. 1:10; cf. Mark 16:2); that is, after the synagogue service, on the first day of the week in commemoration of Jesus's resurrection (cf. Rev. 1:18). Those early Christians, like the Jews, began the day in the evening and often continued their service until dawn (Acts 20:11), as Pliny also intimated. I have elsewhere demonstrated that the early Christian liturgical gathering was a nighttime practice.[19] I have also shown that the primitive Christians had an ecclesiastical calendar, adapted from Judaism, consisting of special days, months, seasons, years, specifically the Sabbath, new moon, Pesach, Omer, Shavuoth, Succoth, Christmas, Sunday, Easter.[20]

The place of the Christian assembly has already been shown as private homes, particularly those of well-to-do members which had

---

[19]Cabaniss, *Liturgy and Literature*, 30-36.

[20]Ibid., 23, 28.

more space (cf. Philem. 2, 22).[21] The Apocalypse suggests that some meetings may have taken place in cemeteries, perhaps over the tombs of martyrs (Rev. 6:9; 8:3; 9:13; 16:7).[22] Even Pliny and Justin, although not explicit, given an impression of open-air services, at least on occasions involving baptisms.

The assembly itself had an orderly arrangement with people in their particular ranks. That is implied by James[23] and the Apocalypse.[24] The major order was the differentiation of clergy and laity, for the early church had from its beginning made that distinction (Gal. 2:9; 6:6; 1 Thess. 5:12; 1 Cor. 4:1; 12:27; Phil. 1:1; Rom. 16:1; 1 Tim 3:1; 5:3, 17; Heb. 13:17; etc.).[25]

Standing with arms uplifted was probably the attitude of prayer (Rev. 20:12; 1 Tim. 2:8), following Jewish practice. There may have been some bowing (Phil. 2:10) and some prostration (Rev. 4:10), but apparently no kneeling. Lights were necessary because of the nighttime (Acts 20:7) and the employment of incense may be intimated (2 Cor. 2:14-16; cf. Rev. 5:8). Triumphal display is suggested (2 Cor. 2:14), as are "splendor" (1 Cor. 3:7-11) and "mystery" (2 Cor. 4:3-4); and Paul alludes to *visual* representations of some sort, perhaps describing the Eucharist (Gal. 3:1), reminding us of the dramatic words of Apuleius cited above, "I saw the sun at midnight, gleaming with bright light."[26] It may be that it was the appeal of Christian liturgy that attracted followers away from "Pagan worship, under that Southern sun, which must have been . . . pic-

---

[21]R. M. Grant, *Early Christianity and Society* (San Francisco: Harper and Row, 1977) 80, 99, 127, for further indications of well-to-do members among early Christians; also Kilpatrick, *The Origins of the Gospel According to St. Matthew*, 125-26.

[22]Yrjö Hirn, *The Sacred Shrine* (London: Macmillan, 1912; originally published in Swedish, 1909) 13-47.

[23]Cabaniss, "Note on Jacob's Homily," 222.

[24]Cabaniss, *Liturgy and Literature*, 47.

[25]Ibid., 22, 28.

[26]Apuleius, *Metamorphoses* 11.23.

turesque."[27] It may have been the Christian liturgy that emptied Pliny's pagan temples and impoverished his pagan festivals.

Several points may be stated in conclusion. From what we have observed there seems to be no clear evidence that there was any singing in the New Testament Christian liturgy and certainly no "general confession" of sins during it. They, like baptism, may have been performed at small separate gatherings, apart from the official service of instruction and Eucharist, or preceding it, as suggested by Pliny and Justin Martyr. Prayer was apparently not offered in the presence of unbelievers (cf. Matt. 6:5-6),[28] but reading of Scripture and exhortation were open to all the curious. The sacraments were, of course, restricted to the faithful. Although some New Testament references to the Eucharist imply that it was celebrated during or after a meal, there is no certain evidence that the meal was a so-called "love feast" (*agape*) or that any part but the Eucharist was a sacred action.

---

[27]Coulton, *Medieval Panorama*, 15.

[28]Note, e. g., the collection of prayers assembled by Donald Coggan, *The Prayers of the New Testament* (Washington: Corpus Books, 1967).

CHAPTER 6

THE BIBLICAL MYSTERY
OF THE SACRAMENTS

IN CHRISTIAN BELIEF THE SACRAMENTS are tangible, palpable, external, visible rites enjoined by Jesus. Yet in the New Testament they are endowed with mysterious efficacy, producing results on human bodies and also on the human spirit. How that can be so is left unexplained even when it is asserted.

Baptism

Although Paul claimed that he was not commissioned to baptize, he nonetheless did so (1 Cor. 1:14, 16-17; cf. Acts 16:33). And although a desultory effort was made to gloss over the fact, Jesus, too, baptized (John 3:22, 26; 4:1-2). It is, therefore, noteworthy that the Christian rite of baptism secured a place of paramount importance in the church and in the New Testament. As the doorway into the Christian community, it was the means of initiation into God's kingdom (Matt. 16:19; John 3:5; 1 Cor. 12:13; Eph. 1:22-23; 4:4-5; Col. 1:13; Rev. 1:5-6, 8; etc.). Just as ceremonial circumcision admitted a male to the old Hebraic covenant, so Christian baptism admitted both male and female to the new covenant (Col. 2:11).

(a) For the person who accepted the rite certain effects ensued. He or she was born (John 3:5) or reborn (Tit. 3:5) to a new kind of life. In baptism one laid aside the old self (Rom. 6:6) and acquired a new self wherein the defaced image of God was restored as if by new creation (2 Cor. 5:17; Eph. 4:24). He was then, according to an oft-repeated Pauline expression "in Messiah" (Rom. 16:7; 1 Cor. 1:30; Col. 1:2; etc.), a condition characterized as having "put on" or having "been clothed with Messiah" (Gal. 3:27).

(b) The same effect of birth or rebirth was also described as death (by crucifixion, Rom. 6:6), burial, and resurrection (Rom. 6:3-5; Col. 2:12). Baptism was thus a veritable *imitatio Christi* (Eph. 5:1-2; 1 Thess. 1:6), a renovation (Tit. 3:5), a passage from (or through) death to life (John 3:16; 36; 4:14; 6:40; 10:10; 1 John 3:14), indeed to deathlessness (1 Tim. 1:16; 2 Tim. 1:10). It was even suggested in the New Testament that a baptized Christian had ascended or could ascend into the heavens with Messiah (Col. 3:1-4; Heb. 10:19-22).[1]

(c) As intimated in (a) above, baptism was alluded to as a new fiat of creation. It was also compared with Noah's escape with his family through the deluge to a new beginning (1 Pet. 3:20-21) and with the Israel's exodus from Egypt through the Reed Sea (1 Cor. 10:1-2). All those earlier events involved water as did baptism: the primeval waters over which God's Spirit brooded (Gen. 1:2), the torrential rains that engulfed all except those in the ark (Gen. 17:12-23), and the miraculously divided sea (Exod. 14:21-22).

(d) Baptism was expressly depicted as an instrument of salvation (John 3:5; Eph. 5:25-26; Tit. 3:5; 1 Pet. 3:21; Mark 16:16), by which one was infused with the Holy Spirit (John 1:33; 3:5; Rom. 8:23; 1 Cor. 3:16; 6:9; 12:13; 2 Cor. 1:21-22; 13:13; Gal. 4:6; Eph. 1:13-14), was purified (John 3:15, and elsewhere), was constituted with all other baptized Christians as one body in Messiah (1 Cor. 12:12-13, 27; Eph. 1:23; 4:4; Col. 1:18), and was united with Messiah (see *a* above).

---

[1]On this concept, see references assembled by Jean Daniélou, *Bible et Liturgie* (Paris: Editions du Cerf, 1951) 269; and Morton Smith, *Clement of Alexandria and a Secret Gospel of Mark* (Cambridge MA: Harvard University Press, 1973) 237-48.

This sacrament had as its constituent elements water and administration with a distinctively Christian formula (to differentiate it from other "baptisms") either in the name of the Trinity (Matt. 28:19) or in the name of Jesus (Acts 2:28; 8:16; 10:18; 19:5).[2] By the nature of such an act, it was unrepeatable (Eph. 4:5; Heb. 6:4-6; 2 Pet. 2:20), just as physical birth was once for all (John 3:4). The particular rite to which Jesus submitted, although not "Christian" baptism, was at least partially assimilated to it and as such was described as fulfillment of "all uprightness" (Matt. 3:15).

Synonyms for "being baptized" further explicated its meanings. One was "receiving light" (Heb. 6:14; 10:32), which in the account of Paul's conversion was joined with being "filled with the Holy Spirit" (Acts 9:17). Another was "being washed" and perhaps "being anointed" (John 13:10; 1 Cor. 1:21; 1 John 2:27). Still another synonym may have been "being sealed" (2 Cor. 1:22). Yet another appeared to have been "professed belief" (John 3:15; 36; 6:47; Acts 2:41; 8:12; 13:39, 42; 16:31; 18:8; Mark 16:16).

Although Johannine baptism was based on repentance (Acts 19:4, and often elsewhere), it is significant that Christian baptism was based on belief. Only one instance (Acts 2:38) mentioned repentance before the Christian rite. It is particularly noteworthy that the expression of belief required for baptism could be vicarious as well as personal. For there were several occasions of baptism being administered to a household, even deceased persons, upon the profession of a representative member (Acts 16:15, 23; 18:8; 1 Cor. 1:16; 15:29).

Eucharist

Both baptism and the Eucharist were deemed in the New Testament and primitive church as means of union with Messiah (on baptism, see preceding section; on the Eucharist, John 5:56; 1 Cor. 10:16) and as evidence of Christians constituting one body (1 Cor. 10:17). As baptism was an infusion of the Holy Spirit (see above),

---

[2]Cf. Blackman, *Marcion and His Influence,* 22.

so the Eucharist was a "first installment of the Spirit" (2 Cor. 1:22; Eph. 1:14). But each sacrament with its distinctive elements occurred at different moments in a Christian's life. They were thus clearly differentiated. Whereas baptism was unique, the Eucharist was repeatable, celebrated at least every Sunday (Acts 20:7), possibly every day (Acts 2:46). Baptism was an initiatory rite performed once for all, but the Eucharist was food for constant nourishment as implied by its elements.

In some ways the Eucharist was assimilated to the Jewish Pesach (Mark 14:12 ‖ Matt. 26:17 ‖ Luke 22:7), but it was never entirely identified with it. It was, however, compared with manna ("bread from heaven" or "angel's food") which the Hebrews ate during their wilderness wandering (John 6:31, 49-50; cf. Exod. 16:4; Psalm 78:24-25; Wisd. 16:20). Most of all it was an intimate meal eaten by a band of Christians in which the host was Jesus: it was the "Dominical banquet" (Lord's supper, 1 Cor. 11:20) or the "Master's table" (1 Cor. 10:21). As such it recalled not only its formal institution as portrayed by the synoptic gospels and by Paul (Mark 14:22-25 ‖ Matt. 26:26-29 ‖ Luke 22:17-19; 1 Cor. 11:23-25), but also presumably many other meals shared by Jesus with His followers (cf. Luke 24:35; Acts 1:4).

To participate in the Eucharist required separation from heathen idolatry (1 Cor. 10:21), worthiness (1 Cor. 11:27), awareness of the significance of the rite (11:29), and examination of one's fitness (11:31). A person's unworthy participation was sin (11:27) such as might result in condemnation (11:29). It might indeed lead to severe bodily illness, infirmity, or even death (11:29).

Initially this sacrament was a memorial of Jesus, as suggested by the repeated Pauline phrase, "for remembrance of me" (1 Cor. 11:24-25), but two unhappy restrictions were later placed on those words. *Memorial* has been used in the sense of a monument to someone or something in the past. Actually, however, even the English word can be employed more dynamically, as when citizens send a memorial to their government. In that case they are reminding not themselves but their governors of something vital in the present, on the basis of which they are at that moment making their pleas or even demands. With such a concept it is well to compare Gen. 9:14-16, wherein it is said, in relation to the sign (or "sacrament") of the Noachic covenant (a rainbow), that *God* will remember!

The other fallacy suggests that the eucharistic rite looks only at the death of Jesus. It should, on the contrary, imply not only His death, but also, as the text explicitly reads, *Him,* in all His fullness, His entire life as well as His death, His teachings, resurrection, ascension, and return in glory, if not indeed His preexistence. It must nevertheless be conceded that this second restriction made an appearance in 1 Cor. 11:26, where the apostle told his readers that whenever they participated in the rite they "preached" the Master's death until the end of time. But even so the Eucharist was a proclamation just as much as a sermon was. It may also have been looked upon as a vivid portrayal of the Master's death (Gal. 3:1; note the stress on visual, not oral and aural, perception).

In establishing the rite Jesus was explicit in identifying the species with Himself (Mark 14:22, 24 ‖ Matt. 26:26, 28) and no amount of explaining can "explain away" the clear meaning of His words. How they can be true is a quite different, if not impossible matter to analyze. In the eucharistic discourse of John 6 Jesus's emphasis was even stronger. There He claimed to be the "bread of life" (6:35, 48, 51), the "bread of heaven" (6:32-33), and declared that the person who ate His "flesh" would live for ever, would possess eternal life (6:51, 54; cf. Heb. 6:4).

Bread was the important element of the rite; use of wine seems to have been an afterthought. In fact the ceremony was often designated concisely as the "breaking of bread" with little or no mention of wine (Luke 24:30; Acts 2:42, 46; 20:7, 11; 27:35). It was always accompanied with thanksgiving, hence the name *Eucharist*. Part of the service may (but only may) have been a recital of the institution (cf. 1 Cor. 11:23-26) and other prayers. On the latter, see 1 Tim. 4:5, where the phrase, *dia logou theou kai enteuxeos* (by God's Word and prayer), is verbally related to Justin

Martyr's ambiguous reference to "make Eucharistic" *di' euches lo-gou*.[3]

¶

Many efforts have been expended over a long range of time to elucidate the Biblical mystery of the sacraments. None has been entirely successful; none has been universally satisfactory. It is, therefore, probably the better part of valor (or in this case, of piety) to let the mystery stand in its majesty and solemnity.[4]

---

[3]Justin Martyr, (First) *Apology,* 66; see discussion in ch. 1 above.

[4]Since preparing the foregoing chapter, I have received a copy of G. D. Kilpatrick, *The Eucharist in Bible and Liturgy* (New York: Cambridge University Press, 1983). His thoroughgong scriptural definition of sacrifice and its application to the Eucharist; his evidence about the Eucharist as an intimate meal restricted to the Christian community; and his demonstration that repetition of the Eucharistic narrative implied a definite structure of the sacrament—with all those points I heartily agree. I dissent only from Kilpatrick's assumption that the earlier part of worship is outside the sacred sphere and his repeated terminology about leaving that portion and "migrating" into the holy sphere of the Eucharist prayer. On the contrary, I believe that the entire Christian service of worship—both liturgy of the Word and liturgy of the sacrament—is well within the realm of the "holy." See the following chapter.

CHAPTER 7

WHAT HAPPENS
AT WORSHIP
A SUMMARY

IN ORDER TO HAVE A PICTURE of Christian worship, we must make a careful definition of it. It is not, for instance, to be confused with Christian activity and good works, necessary and meritorious as they are. It is not to be identified with pious attitudes and feelings, important as they are. It is not to be mistaken for private devotion, basic as that is. It is not to be confounded with instruction, needful as that is. Christian worship may be intimately and inextricably associated with all the preceding matters, as well as with others unmentioned, but we must distinguish it from them in order to understand and define it.

In an earlier day part of Christian worship was known as *opus Dei* (God's work), something done, initiated by God and required by Him. One has only to read the books of Exodus, Leviticus, and Psalms to observe how God wanted His ancient people to worship Him. In those accounts they were told in detail what the content of their worship should be, where it should be, when it should be. The author of the letter to the Hebrews in the New Testament wrote (quoting Exod. 25:40) that the Mosaic tent of worship was but a copy and shadow of the heavenly sanctuary (Heb. 8:5; cf. 8:2, 9:34, 10:1).

Similarly the book of Revelation indicates that specifically Christian worship is a part of, an earthly expression of, a participation in, the endless worship of God in heaven (e.g., Rev. 5:8, 11, 13).

Christian worship, therefore, is a fact, an *opus operatum*, an action, something objective and axiomatic, to be done in and of itself, regardless of extraneous circumstances. It is to be done with relentless regularity (cf. the fourth commandment: Exod. 20:8-11, Deut. 5:12-15), for as St. Augustine has written, "To pray without ceasing [cf. 1 Thess. 5:17] is to pray at regular intervals." It is a way of expressing "the chief end of man" by declaring God's glory and giving Him joy for ever (cf. Ps. 22:3). At first glance it may not seem "relevant" (whatever the meaning of that overused term), but if mediatorial intercession means anything, worship is always significant. A story out of the history of God's ancient people is a parable of its value (Exod. 17:8-13). A day-long battle between Israel and Amalek was taking place in the valley, but by God's appointment the course of battle was determined by Moses on a nearby hill, holding up in his hands the rod of God, supported by his brother Aaron and brother-in-law Hur.

One of the most important things to note about Christian worship is that it is communal. No matter how few the number of worshippers, we pray in community. Our prayers are in the plural. We say, "Our" Father, give "us" this day "our" daily bread, forgive "us our" sins, lead "us" not into temptation, deliver "us" from the evil one (Matt. 6:9-13). We are one with all God's people throughout the world. Moreover we are also joined in worship by all God's people throughout all time, for we are taught that "we are surrounded" by a "great cloud of witnesses" who without us will not be made perfect (Heb. 11:40, 12:1). William Walsham How's great hymn, "For all the saints," is a magnificent expression of this. We are also told that angels are present (1 Cor. 11:10), that our worship somehow mingles with that of angels and archangels in eternal praise (Rev. 5:4). At this point I always think of the delightful verses by Bert Penny, entitled "Attendance Report."

They asked of Johnnie, the acolyte
   Smiling their mockery:
"How many were there, as the day broke bright,
   For Holy Liturgy?"

Johnnie, the acolyte, made reply.
   "Beyond all count," said he,
"Filling the earth and the dawn-rose sky
   As waters fill the sea;

"Angels and archangels, light impearled,
   In Heaven's whole company;
All faithful people around the world;
   And old Miss Jones and me."[1]

But—above all and towering over any other consideration—God Himself is present according to His promise: wherever, whenever two or three are assembled in His name, He is there (Matt. 18:20).

Concerning the content of Christian worship, we find nothing set forth in such detail as in the Old Testament. But St. Paul in Rom. 10:14 offers a clear summary in a series of rhetorical questions which can be arranged in chronological sequence. The service begins with announcement of the mighty acts and words of God in solemn readings of Sacred Scripture, followed by adoring expressions of faith in and acceptance of God's revelation, culminating in communion with God by prayer and Eucharist. The earliest unequivocal description of Christian worship by Justin Martyr (ca. A.D. 150) conforms to Paul's outline.

Converting that outline into musical terms, we may say that worship begins with blasts of trumpets and the roll of kettledrums. They are followed by ringing of bells and pealing of chimes, subsiding into a concert of stringed instruments, but concluding with tympani and trumpets. Converting it into dance, we may say that it begins with the sharp, staccato beat of Spanish flamenco, followed by an exciting Viennese waltz, then falling into a homely American square dance. Or we might convert it into three hymns:

[1]*The Living Church* 133 (18 November 1956): 11.

first, "Joy to the world, the Lord is come," a version of Psalm 98, to the rousing tune "Antioch" by Handel; secondly, "Jesus Christ is risen today, Alleluia," to the stirring tune "Eastern Hymn" with its fourfold repetition of the ancient Hebrew acclamation; and thirdly, "Heralds of Christ, who bear the King's commands," to the tune "National Hymn" sung with trumpet notes. Or we might convert it into Psalms 98, 148, and 72.

On the face of it the foregoing outline looks like a version of Hegelian thesis, antithesis, and synthesis, but with a difference. The first element is indeed a thesis. It is God's own revelation in Scripture: His mighty works of creation and providence, a record of the birth, life, teaching, death, resurrection, and ascension of Messiah Jesus, as well as His intercession at the Father's right hand, His return in glory, and final judgment. It is also an account of the mighty works of the Holy Spirit in the church and sacraments. The second, however, is not antithesis so much as response or reaction. It is acknowledgement by hearers of God's Word, of their belief, by means of creeds and acclamations of praise—in such expressions as the ancient *Amen* (e.g., 2 Cor. 1:20), *Maranatha* (1 Cor. 16:22), *Kyrie eleison,* and *Hosanna* (Ps. 118:25; cf. Mark 11:9f.)—all signifying hearty acceptance. And the third facet is a resolution or, to some degree, a synthesis. It is communion of believers with God: in surrender to Him by oblation of self and possessions, in expression of unworthiness before Him, in thanksgiving, supplication, intercession, and especially in Eucharist.

It is worth noting that there is no real "preparation" for worship (except, of course, baptism, a prerequisite for it). The Word of God simply breaks upon hearers just as it broke upon primeval darkness and silence with the command, "Let there be light" (Gen. 1:3), at which "the morning stars sang together, and all the sons of God shouted for joy" (Job 38:7). The Word of God simply breaks upon hearers as the Gospel burst upon humble Judean shepherds watching their flocks by night (Luke 2:4-5); as God revealed Himself to the unaware and sleeping Jacob at Bethel (Gen. 29:12-19). Similarly there is no true "conclusion" to Christian worship even though its human voice temporarily subsides, for the praise offered by angels goes on forever in heaven. The entire service is in itself a benediction as well as an invocation.

It is easy enough to imagine such worship in our great medieval and modern structures, with trained choirs, and many-voiced organs. But we must remember that worship as we have described it originated among small groups of people, "not many wise, not many powerful, not many noble" (1 Cor. 1:26), who met in their houses, without musical instruments, without skilled singers, without any of the furnishings that we ordinarily associate with worship, even without—strange as it may seem—the full range of Scripture as we have it. Moreover most of their meetings had to take place at night because they were workers with no Sunday "off," and because they were often in peril.

How could a handful of people without a specially built edifice, with only a few persons literate enough to read whatever segments of the Bible they had, with no way to sing in an organized fashion, with no common reading material (if they could read), how could such a handful of people partake of such worship as we have described? It is well to remind ourselves of the enormous and almost incredible ability of people of an earlier world to memorize what was delivered to them orally. In fact, as late as the fourth century St. Augustine is credited with the saying, "Let memory be your book."

It is probable that much prayer was in a bidding or litany form: a leader making the various petitions and the congregation answering at appropriate intervals with short fixed responses. The term *Amen* is well attested (e.g., 2 Cor. 1:20), as also *Hallelujah* (e.g., Rev. 19:4). *Maranatha* has some attestation (1 Cor. 16:22, Rev. 22:20, *Did.* 10:6). Perhaps the Psalm response, "His mercy lasts for ever" (Ps. 136), was employed, as was *Hosanna* (Ps. 118:25; cf. Mark 11:9-10). Very early also appeared *Kyrie eleison* (Lord, have mercy). All of them could be used as responses in prayer as well as acclamations. And surely the Matthean version of the Lord's prayer was available for public use as we know it was for private use (Matt. 6:9-13, *Did.* 8:2-3.).

Above all, one should recall the high esteem in which early Christians held the church. To them it was, indeed *they* were, "God's fellow workers . . , God's field, God's building" (1 Cor. 3:9), "God's temple" with the Holy Spirit dwelling in them (1 Cor. 3:16-17). They believed they were (it was) the very body of Christ (1 Cor. 12:27), God's true Israel (Gal. 6:16), "the pillar and bulwark of truth" (1 Tim. 3:15). They believed that the church was the bride of Messiah and that the Holy Spirit and the church spoke with one voice (Rev. 22:16).

Later, when music, never entirely forgotten, reentered the church's worship, it came as Psalmody at certain "moments" in the service. Psalms were sung at the beginning; Psalms interspersed the long readings of Scripture; Psalms accompanied the offertory of possessions; Psalms "covered" reception of the Eucharistic elements; Psalms ended the worship. By the time peace came to the church singing and other music was very much a part of worship, but the basic outline remained the same as it was in the days of the Apostles.

We can, therefore, imagine the impact of worship on those small, closely knit companies of Christians gathered in a restricted area that was lighted by candles or oil lamps (Acts 20:8), as, without any of the external trappings of music, stained-glass windows, and formal dress, they met as God's people, on God's day, in God's place, to hear Him, acknowledge Him, and communicate with Him. They met not to experience something psychologically impressive or emotionally exciting or esthetically beautiful or mystically elevating or even edifyingly instructive. They met to "do this" in obedience to the command of the Lord at His last supper. They met to join with each other, with the whole church throughout all ages, with angels and archangels and all the hosts of heaven—to worship God.

We can imagine how that worship formed their lives and strengthened them to overcome an alien world of evil spirits, sinful surroundings, malicious neighbors, and a hostile government. As "plain" as some may suppose such worship was, it was never a stark simplicity, but a warm, exilarating *action* that made those early Christians willing to face either an uncertain continued existence or certain death with strange equanimity and with awareness that "the Lord God omnipotent reigns" (Rev. 19:6), that His Word endures for ever (Ps. 119:89; Isa. 40:8), and that only His will is inevitable (Matt. 6:10; Acts 21:4).

EPILOGUE

IF LITURGY IN GENERAL IS, as Eric Werner has written, "a no-man's land between the realms of folklore and art,"[1] Christian liturgy in particular is also an area impinging upon (or impinged upon by) the realms of literature, history, theology, and Biblical studies.[2] It has never lost contact, however, with its etymological and political origin, a "public work," something done by (or for) people. In practice the word is employed to indicate the official action of God's people assembled on God's day (or days) in God's place to perform the duty God has enjoined upon them. It has been restricted to the special duty embodied in the Dominical command, "Do this" (1 Cor. 11:24-25), but it has also been expanded to include the broader kaleidoscope of words and ceremonies closely related to that rite. Today the word is often used in both senses.

A study of Christian liturgy seeks to show it emanating from primitive church practice revealed in the New Testament. As the canon of New Testament Scriptures emerged (according to believers) under guidance of the Holy Spirit, so also (according to believ-

---

[1]Werner, *Sacred Bridge,* 263.

[2]Hirn, *Sacred Shrine,* passim; Adolph Franz, *Die Messe im deutschen Mittelalter* (Darmstadt: Wissenschaftliche Buchgesellschaft, 1963; originally published 1902) passim.

ers) the liturgy emerged under the same aegis. It is, therefore, fitting to return over and over again to study the roots of Christian worship, as we have done in the foregoing treatment. It is not merely a historical curiosity; it is also a concern to Christians in the present day in order to understand the norm by which current liturgy can be judged.

A LITURGICAL
STRUCTURE
FOR TODAY

FROM THE ERA OF THE APOSTLES to Justin Martyr, about a century, the outline of Christian liturgy was essentially the same. In the New Testament we found the order as scriptural lection and homily, prayers and the Eucharist. By the days of Justin the scriptural lections were "lengthy" and probably at least twofold (both Testaments). In Justin the prayers after the homily were also twofold, intercessory and Eucharistic, broken into those two parts by the holy kiss and an "offertory" procession. It would appear that by Justin's time the Eucharist was already disjoined from a preceding supper and therefore required the special act of bringing forward the elements of bread, wine, and water. The separation may have been true as early as Paul (cf. 1 Cor. 11:22).

The primitive Christian liturgy was basically quite straightforward and direct, albeit full of "mystery." But it was blunt and abrupt. Almost inevitably additions would be made at certain "moments," points at which Psalmody, for example, would be introduced into the service. The beginning and end especially seemed to require some expansions to smooth and soften the performance. So there developed the singing of Psalms, hymns, or canticles as the congregation assembled (or at the entry of the ministrants) and a formal dismissal (perhaps accompanied by singing) to indicate close of the service. Singing also eased the monotony of extended readings of Scripture. It would also serve to "cover" the procession with the elements. Those are the main places at which, probably after Justin Martyr, singing became an integral part of Christian liturgy, as we observe from later practice. In Western Europe at a still later period the opening Psalmody came to be called the Introit; Psalm verses interspersing scriptural readings, the Gradual and Alleluia; and at the procession, the Offertory. Unfortunately it also led to multiplication of short prayers (collects) for those special "moments," often detracting from the solemnity of the "great" prayer.

Further passage of time, after the peace of the church, brought diminution of a clear division of the service into two parts, the presumption being by then that all persons present at liturgy were faithful believers. Thereafter, for all practical purposes, came gradual disappearance of popular participation in Eucharistic Communion. The sixteenth-century Reformation sought to restore both to the usual Sunday service, but with little success. The sermon became the great "moment" of the service and eucharistic Communion an occasional practice.

If we consider the sermon and its immediate concomitants as *instruction* and the Eucharist and its concomitants as *worship* (in the narrow sense of the word), we have in effect returned to the ancient twofold division, but with a difference. Instruction became primary and "worship" secondary. Among Protestants the modern liturgical movement has tried to make the usual Sunday service "eucharistic" even if the Eucharist is not celebrated. But that leaves the sermon somewhat embarrassingly ambiguous or anomalous.[1]

In attempting resolution of the difficulty, some words should be sharply distinguished for the sake of clarity. *Worship* (defined in the next paragraph) should not be confused with *devotions*. The

---

[1]Cabaniss, "Place of the Sermon at Liturgy."

latter word should be restricted to describe a person's private prayers and meditation, or perhaps a small group's prayers, meditations, and hymnody. *Instruction* should be exactly what it is in its essential meaning, that is, teaching and learning through homily or address, mutual catechesis (credal forms, etc.), and communal hymnody, with stress on doctrinal and ethical content. *Work,* the praiseworthy activity of God's people in such areas as evangelism, administration of charities, stewardship, and missions, is (or should be) an outcome of worship and under its influence, but not confused with it.

If, therefore, we make those distinctions, we can identify *worship* (liturgy). It is the assembling of God's people, on the Lord's day (and other occasions), in a place to hear God's Word in Scripture, to utter praise for His mercies, to make solemn profession of the Faith, to offer to God the prayers of the whole Christian community, and (if possible) to participate in the Eucharist in obedience to Messiah's command recorded by Paul, "Do this as my memorial" (1 Cor. 11:24-25). *Worship,* in this sense, eventuates in *work;* it informs private *devotions;* and it is made meaningful by careful *instruction.* Even when it tragically lacks the sacramental action, worship (liturgy) should always be eucharistic, that is, thankful, grateful, exultant, exciting, inspiring. It should be in truth a celebration.

Penitential services with confession of sins should be separate from the ordinary Sunday service in order not to dampen the jubilant enthusiasm of worship.[2] Baptism should take place before, not during, eucharistic worship to remind us that it is a prerequisite for such worship. Prayer services and song services for special non-eucharistic occasions, should be clearly separate. If time and place are limited, the foregoing could precede the regular service in a section of the place of meeting different from its central position. Instruction or homily could be offered to a more interested group

---

[2]H. G. Hageman, "Old and New in *The Worshipbook*," *Theology Today* 31 (1974): 207-13, a useful critique.

after the service at a different location (even if in the same room), in order to distinguish it from worship. But instruction should accordingly be de-formalized and restored to its simpler, original, "conversational" style and content, with opportunity for questions and additions, even for disagreements.

However banal the statement, times change and we cannot expect any order or system to be able to withstand alteration. If we should, for example, take the New Testament to be an absolute source of Christian liturgy, the very first thing we would have to get rid of is the New Testament itself! If, like some groups, we should insist on eliminating instrumental music from the church, neither should we have any music, vocal or instrumental. If we should believe in singing only the inspired Psalms, we would have to abandon metrical versions of those Psalms, which no one considers inspired, which are indeed merely paraphrases, not translations. If we depended solely on the New Testament we might have to give up Sunday as the day of worship and revert to Saturday (the Sabbath), for there is precious little hard evidence in the New Testament to justify Sunday observance. If we made the New Testament our only norm of worship, we would have to surrender our church buildings. If the New Testament were absolute in such matters, we might have to restore the ministries of "prophets" (Acts 21:10; etc.), "angels" of the churches (Rev. 2:1; etc.), widows (1 Tim. 5:3-11; etc.), and deaconesses (Rom. 16:1) in a much more elaborate hierarchy than that of bishops (presbyters) and deacons. And we would have to accept an uncertain tradition of oral transmission of the gospel.[3]

But we can adopt and adapt the church's witness which allows for development. Even the liturgy of a radical reformer like Huldreich Zwingli retained a faint shadow of the Mass.[4] His somewhat

---

[3]See comments on this by Oscar Cullmann, *The Early Church,* ed. A. J. B. Higgins (Philadelphia: Westminster Press, 1956) 89, 96.

[4]G. R. Potter, *Zwingli* (Cambridge: University Press, 1978; originally published 1976) 208; Nathaniel Micklem, ed., *Christian Worship* (Oxford: Claren-

less radical successor, John Calvin, characterized his service as "se-lon la coutume de l'Eglise ancienne" (according to the usage of the primitive church).[5] Thus the progression from apostolic practice to Justin Martyr, perhaps even later, was valid. As we have seen, it was a natural, orderly, even inevitable growth. Singing, for example, has become entrenched since early days and the Eucharist has long since been dissociated from a preceding meal. We do change—necessarily and legitimately.

It becomes proper, therefore, to consider what might be the structure of a "New Testament" liturgy for today. What follows is as close to New Testament procedure and content as possible, allowing for some additions from postapostolic periods which at this late date cannot be avoided, certainly not reversed.

Preliminary Remarks

Before the service baptism may be administered on suitable occasions. If a penitential expression is desired or the singing of several songs is appropriate, such may be introduced at this point.

I

The service proper may open with reading or singing one or more Psalms (or hymns). *Gloria in excelsis, Gloria Patri, Christus vincit,* the long-meter Doxology, *Trisagion,* or *Kyrie* could be used (the last two are not, as in some modern liturgies, expressions of penitence, but great acclamations like the first four[6]). This part of the liturgy should be jubilant praise in honor of God and His Word. A brief prayer (collect) has become customary to conclude this section, but it is really not apt.

---

don, 1938) 137-53 (essay by C. J. Cadoux on Zwinglian worship). Although both Potter and Cadoux assigned the Nicene Creed to Zwingli's liturgy, it was in fact the Apostles' Creed that he employed.

[5]Micklem, ed., *Christian Worship,* 154-71 (essay by J. S. Whale on Calvin's liturgies). See also Old, *The Patristic Roots of Reformed Worship,* passim.

[6]See, e. g., M. J. Hatchell, *Commentary on the American Prayer Book* (New York: Seabury Press, 1980) 319-20.

Note. If a Psalm is used at this point, it should not be one of the following which belong more appropriately to other places of the liturgy: Psalms 6, 32, 38, 51, 102, 130, 143 (the penitential Psalms which belong to occasions for confession of sins); Psalms 20 and 67 (which may accompany the dismissal); Psalm 119 (parts of which may follow Old Testament readings); and Psalms 104-106, 111-113, 115-117, 135, 146-150 (the Hallelujah Psalms) which may precede readings of the gospel.

II

(1) A lesson from the Old Testament may be read, preferably according to an approved lectionary.

(b) It could be followed by a section or sections of Psalm 119, said or sung, or a hymn or canticle.

III

(a) A passage from the epistles, Acts, or Revelation may then be read (according to an approved lectionary).

(b) It should be followed by one of the Hallelujah Psalms, said or sung (or as in Zwingli's service, by *Gloria in excelsis*), as a great doxology to greet the gospel reading with appropriate honor and reverence.

IV

A passage from the gospels should then be read (according to an approved lectionary) with great solemnity.

V

A profession of the Faith may be employed (the Apostles' Creed or the Nicene is appropriate, especially the latter). This credal statement may be looked upon either as an act of belief in God's Word just read or as a summary of it. It may also be considered as an expression of the unity of all believers and thus equivalent to the kiss of peace. It may, therefore, be a backward glance at the earlier part of the service or a forward glance at that which is to follow.

VI

The "great prayer" should be inclusive of all the elements of prayer (adoration, acknowledgement of sin, intercession, supplication, thanksgiving, communion of saints). If it is also the eucharistic prayer, it should contain memorial of the institution, invocation of God's blessing upon the elements and worshippers, and offering of both worshippers and elements as a spiritual sacrifice to God. This comprehensive prayer may be divided by the people's acclamations, said or sung, such as *Sanctus, Benedictus qui venit,* and multiple Amens. It should be followed by the communal offering of the Lord's Prayer.

VII

The eucharistic action includes breaking the blessed bread together with distribution of it and the blessed wine for the people's Communion. All should be done decorously in solemn silence, without any diversion by music or otherwise. It may be followed by a brief prayer of thanksgiving.

VIII

The end of the service may be indicated by a Psalm, hymn, or canticle, and a blessing or other form of dismissal.

Concluding Observations

1. *The Sermon.* Omission of reference to sermon/homily above allows us to give it special note here, because the homily/sermon is still the chief means of instruction in the church. It should be introduced aptly at any one of several points in the foregoing liturgy. It could be put after any one of the scriptural readings as deemed suitable: there must be flexibility. The most satisfactory location, however, is after VIII above; or, if the Eucharist is not celebrated, in place of it as VII. See my discussion in "Place of the Sermon at Liturgy" (in the bibliography below).

By late twentieth century sermons have become a significant feature even in the most liturgical churches. The rubrics of the 1977

Book of Common Prayer, in fact, intimate a sermon for virtually all services. In the minds of most laymen a service is inconceivable without a sermon—although they may pay little attention to it. If by chance they do notice it, it is with a shrugging of shoulders suggesting that, after all, they should perhaps wear a hair shirt occasionally, as some primitive ascetics did! I am reminded of a remark by the late Erwin Panofsky: "For reasons insufficiently explored by anthropologists, Americans seem to be genuinely fond of listening to lectures."[7]

The earliest characterization of a sermon at Christian liturgy occurs in the *(First) Apology* of Justin Martyr in connection with what is the earliest unequivocal description of Christian liturgy. Justin commented that after the readings of Scripture the *proestos* (president) made a discourse admonishing (cf. 1 Thess. 5:12) and urging imitation of those good examples mentioned in the readings (ch. 67).

The Greek and Latin terms which give us the words *homily* and *sermon* have as a basic meaning *conversation.* Even the abbreviated versions of "sermons" in the book of Acts look very much like running comments on scriptural passages accompanied by exhortation. And, of course, the so-called sermon on the mountain (or in the plain) is not properly speaking a sermon, but a compilation of scattered sayings assembled by the evangelists.

By the time of later books of the New Testament another influence was at work, namely, the Graeco-Roman rhetorical tradition and Hellenistic Stoic-Cynic diatribes; that is to say, formal oratorical examples and principles, especially the instruction provided, for example, by Quintilian (ca. A.D. 35-95) in his *Institutio oratoria.* The "letter" of James indeed appears to be modeled on such examples and principles, although it is not far away from the simple admonition and exhortation indicated by Justin Martyr. The epistolary form seems in fact to have had more influence on early Christian sermons than Quintilian's rules.

---

[7]*Meaning in the Visual Arts* (Garden City NY: Doubleday, 1955) 332.

In any case the earliest Christian sermon was probably an easy-going "conversational" exposition of Scripture, perhaps concluding with an exhortation. It certainly was not a highly structured disquisition, logically organized, with periodic sentences and stirring peroration, such as we might find in a formal essay or Ciceronian oration.

2. *The collection*, a practical necessity in modern churches, may be inserted after V above or, if there is no celebration of Eucharist, after VI. In any case it should be done quietly, unobtrusively, and in silence; or if appropriate, during the singing of a Psalm, hymn, or canticle, or special music. Theoretically there should be no prayer in connection with it: the collection should not be "glamorized."

3. If singing is not practicable, I, IIb, IIIb, and VIII could be accomplished as antiphonal or responsorial reading of Psalm, hymn, or canticle.

4. The *posture* of worshippers should be reverent. It seems appropriate to stand during the Hallelujah Psalm, reading of the gospel, and recitation of the creed. Otherwise, local custom or devotional habits could provide suitable suggestions. An attempt should be made to avoid too much "bobbing" up and down in the service. It would be better to stand for several parts, then to sit for several parts. There is, moreover, no reason why everyone should act in precisely the same way: freedom, not regimentation, should prevail.[8]

5. Two points have been made above, namely that Scripture should be read in accordance with an approved lectionary and that it should be read "solemnly." There exists already a common lectionary widely adopted by several denominations. A lectionary prevents the readings from being too subjectively selected and from being unnecessarily repetitive. It also provides for the total range of Scripture to be covered in a period of time. There is no need to belabor this point.

---

[8]E. A. Bear, Jr., "The Moods and Modes of Worship," *Theology Today* 31 (1974): 220-27.

On the other hand, "solemnity" in the public reading of Scripture does seem to require some further explanation. By that word I mean, of course, audibly, not mumbled; and intelligibly (even intelligently), not with irritating, inexcusable mispronunciations and false emphases. As a consequence, responsive and unison attempts do not seem to me to constitute "solemn" reading. They belong to Psalmody and praise, to credal statements, and to a few prayers (litanies, the Lord's Prayer, etc.).

6. *The hour* of worship should be flexible. No sanctity adheres to eleven o'clock on Sunday morning. A laudable current practice is return to the ancient observance of a vigil in late afternoon or "eve," with the same dignity as a morning service. In many cases today that would seem to be quite practical. It would also seem convenient to have a number of services on the Lord's day so that worshippers could have some choice of the time at which they could attend in fulfillment of their obligation.

7. If more than one ministrant takes part in the liturgy, the chief celebrant (pastor) should always open and close the service. In consecration of the eucharistic elements, the action should not be divided: the ministers should "concelebrate," both or all saying the "great prayer" (or at least the critical parts of it).

ONE
FOR THE ROAD

THE EUCHARIST OR LORD'S SUPPER has long been subjected to critical examination from almost every conceivable point of view.[1] Yet
there seems to be one small aspect that has been overlooked, one
which is nonetheless quite apparent in the biblical evidence.

The first description of the Supper is recorded by the Apostle
Paul in 1 Cor. 11:25-26. Although it appears to be an account
straightforward and commonplace enough, it is worth noting that
the ceremonial took place at a *special* meeting. It was not a routine
meal, for the Apostle asks, "Do you not have houses for eating and
drinking" (11:22) and gives specific instruction that "if anyone is
hungry, let him eat at home" (11:34). Even if the Supper was celebrated in a private home, however, it was not an ordinary meal,
but something with particular significance that people did only when
they "met together" and not in their permanent residences (11:20).

One may go a step further by referring to his earlier mention of
the occasion (1 Cor. 10:16). The context of that passage is a hom-

---

[1] The classic treatment is still Hans Lietzmann, *Messe und Herrenmahl: Eine
Studie zur Geschichte der Liturgie,* 3rd ed. (Berlin: Walter de Gruyter, 1955; orig-
inally published 1926) of which the latest edition is *Mass and the Lord's Supper: A
Study in the History of the Liturgy* (for bibliographical details, see ch. 1 n. 1).

iletic retelling of the wilderness wandering of the ancient Israelites (10:1-11), with allusions to crossing the Reed Sea, manna and quails, miraculous provision of water, idolatry, the bronze snake—all recorded, he says, "to instruct us" (10:11). The Eucharist thus evoked recollection of God's older people in the vital experience of their beginnings.

When one turns to the later narratives of the Gospels, he finds there also elements of impermanence. In the Synoptics the disciples did not know where the meal was to be eaten and asked where to make preparation (Mark 14:12; Matt. 26:17; Luke 22:9). Jesus's reply indicated a temporary provision, a (guest?) room in a private house or at an inn (Mark 14:14; Luke 22:11; Matt. 26:18 suggests more clearly a private house). The meal ended, Jesus and His students left the place that had served its purpose (Mark 14:32; Matt. 26:30; Luke 22:39). There is no compelling reason to identify it with the "upstairs room" of Acts 1:13, unless it was part of a tavern, as vaguely intimated by the statement, "where they were staying." In the Johannine account the place of the Supper is unidentified (John 13:1), but there are several references to "leaving" (13:36, 14:3, 5, 16:28) before the company actually did leave (18:1). The inference is a place borrowed or rented for a special occasion.

The obviously eucharistic account of the feeding of five thousand (and its doublet, the feeding of four thousand)[2] fits into the scheme of desert, crisis, and urgency. It follows upon the dramatic and moving execution of the Baptizer John (so Matt., Mark, Luke); it is succeeded by Peter's "great confession" (Luke, John; Matt. places that after the incident of the four thousand) or the miracle of Jesus's walking on water (Mark, Matt).

By the time the Synoptics were written, the eucharistic institution had already been assimilated to the Passover. Whether it was actually related is, of course, a matter of conjecture. But even if, as most likely, it was not a variant of Pesach, the paschal context is

----

[2]Mark 6:30-45; Matt. 14:13-23; Luke 9:10-18; John 6:3-15 (five thousand); Mark 8:1-10; Matt. 15:29-39 (four thousand).

obvious, even obvious in the earlier Pauline documents (e.g., 1 Cor. 5:7-8). Once the Passover association was invoked, it became an important strain in eucharistic thought. All its primitive overtones were educed in the minds of participants. One must therefore turn back to the Old Testament situation.

On the dark night when the angel of death destroyed the Egyptian firstborn, the Israelites were virtually compelled to leave Egypt in haste, in such haste that the dough for their bread was not allowed to rise (Exod. 12:32-33), but had to be hurriedly carried in packs on their shoulders. In the land of Canaan an old agricultural festival of unleavened bread thus coalesced with a historical celebration of escape from Egyptian bondage (Exod. 12:17; Deut. 16:3), and became one of three major festivals of the Jewish religion, indeed *the* feast par excellence.

A sense of urgency and haste, of pilgrimage, journey, and wilderness wandering, and of impermanence thereby penetrated the Christian Eucharist. "This is how you are to eat it: with your loins girt, sandals on your feet, and your staff in hand, you shall eat it like those who are in flight" (Exod. 12:11, NAB). Only a few actual Passovers are recorded in the Old Testament, but those carry the note of urgency.[3]

By New Testament times the festival had become associated with pilgrimage to Jerusalem.[4] Although the original prescriptions made the Passover a private and family affair, it became a period of leaving home, of taking up temporary abode in or near Jerusalem, and of returning therefrom. This development added inevitably to the sense of journey and movement. It added also a sense of danger, because of the possibility of rioting.[5] The Roman government was acutely conscious of that not only as a possibility, but also as an actuality.

---

[3]Num. 9:5-8; Josh. 5:10-12; 2 Kings 23:22-23; 2 Chron. 30-13-26; 35:1-19; Ezra 6:19-20.

[4]Cf. Luke 2:41-42; 23:7; John 2:23; 4:45; 5:1; 11:55; 12:12, 20.

[5]Cf. Mark 15:6; Matt. 27:5, 15; John 18:39.

How all the foregoing impinged upon the Eucharistic observance can be discerned in New Testament references to actual celebrations, the two most notable being in the book of Acts, if they
are indeed historical events. The first (20:7-12) was a nighttime occasion in a third floor upstairs room at Troas. The missionaries had
just escaped a Jewish plot against Paul. The (crowded?) room was
eerily lighted with numerous flickering lamps and candles. The at-
mosphere must have been heavy with warmth and smoke. Then an
accident happened: a drowsy youth fell to the ground from his perch
in a window. Stunned by the steep fall, he nevertheless lived, presumably joined in the Eucharistic rite, and stayed with the band of
believers until "rosy-fingered dawn" broke in the eastern sky.

The second (27:35-36) occurred after a severe storm at sea.
Raging winds, cloudy days, long wintry nights, the tempest-driven
ship adrift in the Adriatic—two hundred and seventy-six people
packed together in close quarters had endured those terrors for two
weeks virtually without food. Then, as a cold, grey, rainy, sunless
morning was about to break, the Apostle Paul celebrated the Eucharist just before the shipwreck and fortunate escape to the island
of Malta.

Later celebrations in cemeteries, catacombs, private dwellings
are well documented. The Eucharist was in reality for several
hundred years a "last" supper. Many would die after it; many would
go to prison; many would have to flee.[6] Even if nothing untoward
happened and they could go again to another Eucharist, there was
always the danger that it might prove to be the "last." The custom
soon arose of providing a dying Christian with the Eucharist under
the term *viaticum,* the last food that a Christian received as he set
forth on his journey to another world.[7]

Observe that the practice was quite true to its history: it was and
is food for a crisis, food for a journey, food for sustenance, food for

---

[6]Gregory Dix, *The Shape of the Liturgy,* passim, esp. 141-55.

[7]Gregory Grabka, "Christian Viaticum: A Study of Its Cultural Background,"
Traditio 9 (1953): 1-43.

life, whether that life is the present or the future. And thus we arrive at an interpretation of the Eucharist as "one for the road"! The English expression usually suggests drink or the stirrup cup, but it is an almost exact translation of the Greek term *ephodion* or Latin *viaticum,* which suggests "provision for a journey."

The preceding interpretation has implications for liturgical practice. The Eucharist should not be characterized as a formal supper, dinner, or banquet; it should be looked upon as one's "last" mouthful just before a journey, whether back into the world or out of it. It should, therefore, like the ancient Passover described in Exod 12:11 (quoted above), be received standing, even walking. Nothing should follow it but departure from the place where it was administered. It is a final act in and of itself before this world or another world engulfs us.

JUSTIN MARTYR
AND
PLINY THE YOUNGER

A translation of Justin Martyr, (First) *Apology* 65-67, analyzed in chapter 1 above.

¶

65. When the person who was convinced expressed his assent, he was baptized [washed]. Then we lead him to the place where those called "brothers" were assembled. Earnest common prayers were offered for themselves, for the "enlightened" one, for all people everywhere. It was prayer that we who have learned the truth and expressed it in deeds may be found as good citizens and keepers of the commandments; also that we may be saved with everlasting salvation. When we have concluded those prayers, we greet each other with a kiss.

At that point bread and a cup of water and of wine-mixed-with-water are brought forward to the "president" of the brothers. He takes them and sends up praise and glory to the Father of all through the name of the Son and of the Holy Spirit. At considerable length he offers Thanksgiving [Eucharist] that we have been made worthy of these things from Him. When he has completed the prayers and the Thanksgiving [Eucharist], all the people present respond resoundingly, "Amen." The word "Amen" is Hebrew for "May it be so."

When the "president" has finished and all the people have made reply, those among us called "deacons" distribute to each of those present for their reception some of the eucharistic bread and wine-and-water. They also carry away some to those who are absent.

66. This food we call "Eucharist." It is not permissible for any one to partake of it except one who believes to be true what he learned from us; one who has been washed with that washing for remission of sins and for regeneration; one who lives in the manner the Messiah has transmitted to us. For we do not receive these elements as ordinary bread and ordinary drink. Just as Jesus Messiah our Savior, made flesh through God's Word, took both flesh and blood for our salvation, so have we also been taught that the food is both flesh and blood of that incarnate Jesus. By a transformation our blood and flesh are nourished by that food, made eucharistic through a formula of prayer that is from Him.

For the apostles, in their memoirs, which are called "gospels," handed down in the following manner what was enjoined upon them. Jesus took bread, gave thanks [made Eucharist], and said, "Do this for memorial of Me; this is My body." In the same way He took the cup, gave thanks, and said, "This is My blood."

To them [the apostles] alone He gave it. But in imitation the evil demons also handed this down to be done in the mysteries of Mithras. You either know or can learn that, in their secret rites of initiation, bread and a cup of water are set forth with certain words said over them.

67. From then on we constantly remind each other of these matters. Those who "have" look after all those who "have not"; and we are always together with each other. Over everything that we receive we bless the Creator of all things through His Son Jesus Messiah and through the Holy Spirit.

On the day called "of Helios" there is a gathering in the same place [or, together] of all those who dwell in cities and countrysides. The memoirs of the apostles or writings of the prophets are read as long as time permits. When the "lector" [reader] has finished, the "president" thereupon delivers an admonition and invitation to imitate those admirable examples. Afterwards we all stand and send up prayers together.

As we noted earlier, when we have ended the prayer, bread and wine-and-water are brought forward. In like manner the "president" sends up prayers and Thanksgivings [Eucharists], as he has the ability. The people respond resoundingly and say the "Amen."

To each person there is distribution and reception of the eucharistic species; and to those who are absent it is sent by the "deacons."

Those who are prosperous and willing donate whatever each one wishes, according to his own decision. The collection is deposited with the "president." He is the one who watches over orphans and widows; over those in want because of sickness or any other reason; over those in prison; and over those strangers sojourning among us. In a word, he is the caretaker of all who are in need.

We all make our assembly on the day "of Helios" since it is the first day. On it God, having transformed darkness and matter, made the cosmos. On it also Jesus Messiah our Savior rose from the dead. It was on the day before that "of Kronos" that they crucified Him and on the day after that "of Kronos," namely, on the day "of Helios" that He appeared to His apostles and disciples and taught them these things which we have transmitted to you for your inspection.

A translation of Pliny the Younger, *Epistolae* 10.96.5-10, analyzed in chapter 2 above.

¶

5. An anonymous pamphlet, containing the names of many [Christians], has come to my attention. Those [named therein] who denied being or having been Christians, I decided to release when, in my presence, they invoked the gods; when they offered prayers, with incense and wine, to your image (which for that purpose I had ordered brought forward along with likenesses of the divinities); and when they cursed Christ [Messiah]. It is said that true Christians cannot be compelled to act in that manner.

6. Others named by the informer declared that they were Christians, but soon renounced [the superstition]. Some of those who had been [Christians] stopped about three years ago; some, many years ago; one, indeed, as many as twenty years ago. All these, too, venerated your image and the likenesses of the gods. They also cursed Christ [Messiah].

7. They affirmed that the substance of their guilt and folly was as follows. They were accustomed to assemble on a fixed day, to utter responsively an incantation to Christ [Messiah] as to a god, and to bind themselves by an oath not to commit any crime (thieveries, banditries, adulteries), not to betray a confidence [perhaps "not to betray the Faith"], not to default on a deposit when called upon for it. When those matters had been transacted, they were in the habit of dividing and coming together again to take an ordinary and harmless food. But they desisted from such practice after my edict, issued in accord with your mandates, forbidding fraternal associations.

8. I deemed it all the more necessary to question under torture two servant girls called *ministrae* [deaconesses?] and extract from them what was the truth. I discovered nothing, however, but a depraved, extravagant superstition.

9. Since the notion is so widespread, I hasten, therefore, to consult you. For it appeared to me a matter worthy of consultation, especially because of the number of those imperilled [by the anonymous pamphlet]. Many of all ages, of all ranks, of both sexes are being called or will be called into danger. Although the contagion of this superstition has permeated not only cities, but also villages, and countrysides, it seems possible to stop it and thwart it.

10. It is certainly more than appropriate for temples, virtually deserted, to be thronged again with crowds and for sacred assemblies, long neglected, to be frequented again, as well as for fatted victims to be brought again to market. Up until now only the rarest purchaser was to be found. It is, moreover, easier to suppose that a multitude of people can be corrected if there is opportunity for repentance.

BIBLIOGRAPHY

The following abbreviations of familiar series and journals are used in the bibliography.

A-NF	The Ante-Nicene Fathers
CBQ	Catholic Biblical Quarterly
CP	Classical Philology
HTR	Harvard Theological Review
JBR	Journal of Bible and Religion
JR	Journal of Religion
LCL	Loeb Classical Library
NTS	New Testament Studies
VG	Vigiliae Christianae

Books

Angus, S. *The Mystery-Religions and Christianity*. New York: Scribner's, 1925.

The Ante-Nicene Fathers. Ed. A. Roberts and J. Donaldson. 2 vols. Buffalo NY: Christian Literature Publishing Co., 1887. Consult for Justin Martyr, *Dialogue with Trypho*, and Tatian, *Ad Graecos*, below.

Apuleius. *The Golden Ass (Metamorphoses)*. Trans. W. Adlington; rev. S. Gaselee. LCL. London: Heinemann, 1919; first published 1915.

Bacchiocchi, Samuele. *From Sabbath to Sunday*. Rome: Pontifical Gregorian University Press, 1977.

Barth, Christoph. *Introduction to the Psalms*. New York: Charles Scribner's Sons, 1966.

Beare, William. *Latin Verse and European Song: A Study in Accent and Rhythm*. London: Methuen, 1957.

Blackman E. C. *Marcion and His Influence*. London: SPCK, 1948.

Cabaniss, Allen. *Liturgy and Literature*. University AL: University of Alabama Press, 1979. See for several reprints noted below.

Philip Carrington. *The Early Christian Church*. 2 vols. Cambridge: University Press, 1957.

_____. *The Primitive Christian Calendar. 1. Introduction and Text*. Cambridge: University Press, 1952.

_____. *According to Mark*. Cambridge: University Press, 1960.

Clement of Rome. *First Letter to the Corinthians*. In Lake, *The Apostolic Fathers*, 1:9-121, below.

Coggan, Donald. *The Prayers of the New Testament*. Washington DC: Corpus Books, 1967.

Coulton, G. G. *Medieval Panorama*. Cambridge: University Press, 1939.

Cross, F. L. *I Peter: A Paschal Liturgy*. London: Mowbray, 1954.

Cullmann, Oscar. *Early Christian Worship*. Trans. A. S. Todd and J. B. Torrance. London: SCM Press, 1954.

_____. *The Early Church*. Trans. A. J. B. Higgins. Philadelphia: Westminster Press, 1956.

Dahood, Mitchell. *Psalms*. 3 vols. Anchor Bible 16, 17, 17a. Garden City NY: Doubleday, 1966, 1968, 1970.

D'Alviella, G. *The Mysteries of Eleusis. The Rites and Rituals of the Classical Greek Mystery Tradition*. Wellingborough UK: Aquarian Press, 1981.

Daniélou, Jean. *Bible et Liturgie*. Paris: Editions du Cerf, 1951.

_____. *Gospel Message and Hellenistic Culture*. Trans. J. A. Baker. London: Darton, Longman and Todd, 1973.

Didache. In Lake, *The Apostolic Fathers*. 1:309-33, below.

Dix, Gregory. *The Shape of the Liturgy*. With additional notes by P. V. Marshall. New York: Seabury Press, 1982; first published 1945.

_____. *Jew and Greek: A Study in the Primitive Church*. London: Dacre Press, 1953.

Enslin, Morton Scott. *The Literature of the Christian Movement*. Part 3 of *Christian Beginnings*. Harper Torchlight Edition. New York: Harper and Brothers, 1956; first published 1938.

Eusebius. *The Ecclesiastical History*. 1. Trans. Kirsopp Lake. 2. Trans. and ed. E. L. Oulton and H. I. Lawlor. LCL. London: Heinemann, 1926, 1932.

Feldman, L. H. See Josephus, *Jewish Antiquities*, below.

Ford, J. Massyngberde. *Revelation*. Anchor Bible 38. Garden City NY: Doubleday, 1973.

Franz, Adolph. *Die Messe im Deutschen Mittelalter*. Darmstadt: Wissenschaftliche Buchgesellschaft, 1963; first published 1902.

Goodspeed, Edgar J. *A History of Early Christian Literature*. Chicago: University of Chicago Press, 1942. See also the 2nd ed. rev. and enlarged by R. M. Grant (1966), same publisher.

Goulder, M. D. *The Evangelists' Calendar, A Lectionary Explanation of the Development of Scripture*. London: SPCK, 1978.

Grant, Robert M. *Ignatius of Antioch*. The Apostolic Fathers: A New Translation and Commentary 4. Camden NJ: Thomas Nelson and Sons, 1966.

_____. *Early Christianity and Society*. San Francisco: Harper and Row, 1977.

_____. *A Historical Introduction to the New Testament*. New York: Harper and Row, 1963.

Guilding, Aileen. *The Fourth Gospel and Jewish Worship*. Oxford: Clarendon, 1960.

Hahn, Ferdinand. *The Worship of the Early Church*. Trans. D. E. Green; ed. John Reumann. Philadelphia: Fortress Press, 1973.

Hatchell, M. J. *Commentary on the American Prayer Book*. New York: Seabury Press, 1980.

Hirn, Yrjö. *The Sacred Shrine*. London: Macmillan, 1912; first published in Swedish 1909.

Hooke, S. H., ed. *Myth, Ritual, and Kingship*. Oxford: Clarendon, 1960. See for articles by Brandon, Rowley, and Widengren, below.

Idelsohn, A. Z. *Jewish Liturgy and Its Development*. New York: Schocken Books, 1972; first published 1932.

Ignatius of Antioch. *Epistles*. In Lake, *The Apostolic Fathers*, 1:173-201, below.

Josephus. *Jewish Antiquities*. Trans. H. St. J. Thackeray, R. Marcus, A. Wikgren, L. H. Feldman. 6 vols. LCL. London: Heinemann, 1930–1955.

——————————. *The Jewish War*. Trans. H. St. J. Thackeray. 2 vols. LCL. London: Heinemann, 1927, 1928.

Justin Martyr. (First) *Apology*. In B. L. Gildersleeve, ed., *The Apologies of Justin Martyr*. New York: Harper, 1877.

——————————. *Dialogue with Trypho*. Trans. in A-NF, 1:194-270, above.

Kilpatrick, G. D. *The Beginnings of the Gospel according to Saint Matthew*. Oxford: Clarendon, 1950; first published 1946.

——————————. *The Eucharist in Bible and Liturgy*. New York: Cambridge University Press, 1983.

Lake, Kirsopp. *The Apostolic Fathers*. 1. LCL. London: Heinemann, 1930; first published 1912. See for Clement of Rome, Ignatius of Antioch, and the *Didache*, above.

Lietzmann, Hans. *Messe und Herrenmahl: Eine Studie zur Geschichte der Liturgie*. 3rd ed. Berlin: Walter de Gruyter, 1955; first published in 1926. English translation: *Mass and Lord's Supper. A Study in the History of the Liturgy*. Trans. D. H. G. Reeve. With introduction and further inquiry by R. D. Richardson. Leiden: Brill, 1979.

Marcus, R. See Josephus, *Jewish Antiquities*, above.

Marshall, P. B. See Dix, *Shape of the Liturgy*, above.

Martin, Ralph P. *Carmen Christi*. Cambridge: University Press, 1967.

——————————. *Worship in the Early Church*. Grand Rapids MI: Eerdmans Publishing Co., 1978; first published 1964.

——————————. *The Worship of God*. Grand Rapids MI: Eerdmans Publishing Co., 1982.

Maxwell, W. D. *John Knox's Genevan Service Book 1556*. Edinburgh: Oliver and Boyd, 1931.

——————————. *An Outline of Christian Worship*. London: Oxford University Press, 1936.

Melton, Julius. *Presbyterian Worship in America*. Richmond VA: John Knox Press, 1967.

Micklem, Nathaniel, ed. *Christian Worship*. Oxford: Clarendon, 1938.

Moulton, R. G. *The Modern Reader's Bible*. New York: Macmillan, 1939.

Old, H. O. *The Patristic Roots of Reformed Worship*. Zürich: Theologischer Verlag, 1975.

_____. *Worship*. Guides to the Reformed Tradition. Atlanta: John Knox Press, 1984.

Panofsky, Erwin. *Meaning in the Visual Arts*. Garden City NY: Doubleday and Co., 1955.

Pater, Walter. *Marius the Epicurean*. London: Macmillan, 1924.

Philo. *Vita Mosis*. In *Philo*, trans. F. H. Colson, 6:276-595. LCL. London: Heinemann, 1935.

Pike, Albert. *Morals and Dogma*. Richmond VA: L. H. Jenkins, 1930; first published 1871.

Pliny the Younger. *Letters*. In S. E. Stout, *Plinius, Epistolae a Critical Edition*. Indiana University Humanities Series 49. Bloomington: Indiana University Press, 1962.

Plutarch. *Table Talks*. In Plutarch, *Moralia* 8. Trans. D. A. Clement and H. B. Hoffleit. LCL. London: Heinemann, 1969.

Potter, G. H. *Zwingli*. Cambridge: University Press, 1978; first published 1986.

Quintilian. *Institutio Oratoria*. 2 vols. Ed. M. Winterbottom. Oxford: Clarendon, 1970.

Reeve, D. H. G. See Lietzmann, above.

Richardson, R. D. See Lietzmann, above.

Robinson, John A. T. *Redating the New Testament*. Philadelphia: Westminster Press, 1975.

_____. *Twelve New Testament Studies*. Naperville IL: Alec R. Allenson, Inc., 1962.

Safrai, S., and M. Stern, eds. *The Jewish People in the First Century*. Philadelphia: Fortress Press, 1976.

Sandmel, Samuel. *A Jewish Understanding of the New Testament*. Cincinnati: Hebrew Union College Press, 1956.

Selwyn, E. G. *The First Epistle of Peter*. 2nd ed. London: Macmillan, 1958.

Shepherd, M. H., Jr., *The Paschal Liturgy and the Apocalypse*. Richmond VA: John Knox Press, 1960.

Sherwin-White, A. N. *The Letters of Pliny: A Historical and Social Commentary*. Oxford: Clarendon, 1966.

Sluis, D. J. van der, et al. *Elke Morgen Nieuw.* Arnhem: B. Folkertsma-Stichung voor Talmudica, 1978.

Smith, Morton. *Clement of Alexandria and a Secret Gospel of Mark.* Cambridge MA: Harvard University Press, 1973.

——————. *Jesus the Magician.* San Francisco: Harper and Row, 1978.

Stern, M. See Safrai, above.

Stout, S. E. *Scribe and Critic at Work in Pliny's Letters.* Indiana University Humanities Series 30. Bloomington: Indiana University Press, 1954.

Suetonius. *Life of Claudius.* In *Suetonius,* trans. J. C. Rolfe, 2:3-183. LCL. London: Heinemann, 1920.

Syme, Ronald. *Tacitus.* 2 vols. Oxford: Clarenden, 1963, from corrected proofs of 1st ed., 1958.

Tacitus. *Annals.* Ed. E. Koestermann. Leipzig: Teubner, 1965.

Tatran. *Ad Graecos.* Trans. in A-NF, 2:65-82 (83), above.

Tertullian. *Apologeticus.* Trans. T. R. Glover. LCL. London: Heinemann, 1931.

Thackeray, H. St. J. See Josephus, *The Jewish War* and *Jewish Antiquities,* above.

Trocmé, E. *The Passion as Liturgy. A Study in the Origin of the Passion Narratives in the Four Gospels.* London: SCM, 1983.

Waite, A. E. *A New Encyclopedia of Freemasonry.* 2 vols. New York: Weathervane Books, 1970.

Werner, Eric. *The Sacred Bridge.* New York: Columbia University Press, 1959.

Wikgren, A. See Josephus, *Jewish Antiquities,* above.

Willoughby, H. R. *Pagan Regeneration.* Chicago: University of Chicago Press, 1929.

Articles

Banckham, Richard. "The Worship of Jesus in Apocalyptic Christianity," NTS 27 (1981): 322-41.

Bean, E. A., Jr. "The Moods and Modes of Worship." *Theology Today* 31 (1974): 220-27.

Bell, A. A. "The Date of John's Apocalypse." NTS 25 (1978): 93-102.

Böcher, Otto. "Johanneisches in der Apocalypse des Johannes." NTS 27 (1981): 310-21.

Brandon, S. G. F. "The Myth and Ritual Position Carefully Considered." In Hooke, *Myth, Ritual, Kingship,* 261-91, above.

Cabaniss, Allen. "Alleluia: A Word and Its Effect." *Studies in English* 5 (1964): 67-74. Reprinted in Cabaniss, *Liturgy and Literature,* 114-21, above.

——————. "A Critical Review of the *Book of Common Worship* (1946)." *Journal of the Presbyterian Historical Society* 26 (1948): 87-100.

——————. "A Critique of 'Service for the Lord's Day'." *Reformed Liturgics* 1 (Fall 1964): 19-24.

——————. "Doctor Mack on the Liturgy." *Presbyterian Survey* 43 (September 1957): 34-35.

——————. "Early Christian Nighttime Worship." JBR 25 (1957): 30-33. Reprinted in Cabaniss, *Liturgy and Literature,* 30-36, above.

——————. "The Harrowing of Hell, Psalm 24, and Pliny the Younger: A Note." VG 7 (1953): 65-74. Reprinted in Cabaniss, *Liturgy and Literature,* 62-71, above.

——————. "In Defense of Liturgy." *Presbyterian Outlook* 146 (15 June 1964): 2.

——————. "Liturgy in the Southern Presbyterian Church." *Union Seminary Review* 54 (1942): 11-27.

——————. "Liturgy-making Factors in Primitive Christianity." JR 23 (1943): 43-58.

——————. "A Note on Jacob's Homily." *Evangelical Quarterly* 47 (1975): 219-22.

——————. "A Note on the Liturgy of the Apocalypse." *Interpretation* 7 (1953): 78-85. Reprinted in Cabaniss, *Liturgy and Literature,* 42-52, above.

——————. "Place of the Sermon at Liturgy." *Reformed Liturgics* 4 (1967): 21-25.

——————. "Shields, the Liturgy, and I." *Presbyterian Survey* 46 (March 1956): 41.

————————. "Wisdom 18:14-15: An Early Christmas Text." VG 10 (1956): 97-102. Reprinted in Cabaniss, *Liturgy and Literature,* 53-57, above.

————————. "The Worship of 'Most Primitive' Christianity." JBR 26 (1958): 318-21. Reprinted in Cabaniss, *Liturgy and Literature,* 21-29, above.

————————. "Worship Tested by History." *Presbyterian Outlook* 137 (15 August 1955): 5-6.

Coulter, C. C. "Further Notes on the Ritual of the Bithynian Christians." CP 35 (1940): 60-63.

Eckman, B. "A Quantitative Metrical Analysis of the Philippians Hymn." NTS 26 (1980): 258-66.

Enslin, Morton Scott. "The Pontic Mouse." *Anglican Theological Review* 27 (1945): 1-16.

Flusser, D. "Paganism in Palestine." In Safrai and Stern, *The Jewish People in the First Century,* 1069-79, above.

Goulder, M. D. "The Apocalypse as an Annual Cycle of Prophecies." NTS 27 (1981): 342-67.

Grabka, Gregory. "Christian Viaticum: A Study of Its Cultural Background." *Traditio* 9 (1953): 1-43.

Grant, Robert M. "Pliny and the Christians." HTR 41 (1948): 273-74.

Hageman, H. G. "Old and New in *The Worshipbook.*" *Theology Today* 31 (1974): 207-13.

Kraemer, C. J. "Pliny and the Early Church Service: Fresh Light from an Old Source." CP 29 (1934): 293-300.

Lewis, P. B. "Indications of a Liturgical Source in the Gospel of Mark." *Encounter* 39 (1978): 385-94.

Mason, D. R. "An Examination of 'Worship' as a Key for Re-examining the God Problem." JR 55 (1975): 76-94.

Mohler. S. L. "The Bithynian Christians Again." CP 30 (1935): 167-69.

Moloney, R. "The Early Eucharist: An Hypothesis of Development." Irish Theological Quarterly 45 (1978): 167-76.

————————. "The Early Eucharist: The Jewish Background." *Milltown Studies* 2 (1978): 1-10.

Penny, Bert. "Attendance Report" (poem). *Living Church* 133 (18 November 1956): 11.

Pritchard, N. M. "Profession of Faith and Admission to Communion in the Light of I Corinthians 11 and Other Passages." *Scottish Journal of Theology* 33 (1980): 55-70.

Rowley, H. H. "Ritual and the Hebrew Prophets." *In Hooke, Myth, Ritual, and Kingship*, 236-60, above.

Schroedel, W. R. "Ignatius and the Archives." HTR 71 (1978): 97-106.

Shepherd, M. H., Jr. "The Early Apologists and Christian Worship." JR 18 (1938): 60-79.

Sigal, Philip. "Early Christian and Rabbinic Liturgical Affinities: Exploring Liturgical Acculturation." NTS 30 (1984): 63-90.

Smith, Morton. "Pauline Worship as Seen by Pagans." HTR 73 (1980): 241-49.

Stanley, D. M. "Carmenque Christo Quasi Deo Dicere . . . ," CBQ 20 (1938): 173-91.

_____. "The Theme of the Servant of Yahweh in Primitive Christian Soteriology." CBQ 16 (1954): 385-425.

Sturdy, John. "Clement, Ignatius and Polycarp: A Revision of Accepted Views" (typescript).

Verheul, A. "La prière eucharistique dans la Didache." *Questions Liturgiques* 60 (1979): 197-207.

Walter, Nikolaus. "Christusglaube und Heidnische Religiosität in Paulinischen Gemeinden." NTS 25 (1979): 422-42.

Widengren, G. "Early Hebrew Myths and Their Interpretation." In Hooke, *Myth, Ritual and Kingship*, 149-203, above.

INDEX
of Biblical References

INDEX
of Authors

*Allen Cabaniss is research
professor of history emeritus,
University of Mississippi.*

MP *Pattern in Early Christian Worship*

Typography designed by Margaret Jordan Brown
Composition by Mercer University Press Composition Department
Cover design by Alesa Jones

Production Specifications:
text paper—50 lb. Glatfelter's Natural; smooth finish
    endpapers—80 lb. Natural
    covers (on .88 boards)—Kivar 9 Bright White Corinth, printed PMS
534 (blue), PMS 256 (purple), and film laminated

Printing (offset lithography) and binding by Braun-Brumfield, Inc., Ann
Arbor MI.